주니어

고릴라 영문법

Junior Gorilla Grammar

level 2

핵심만 반복
그리고 영작!

2,500여 개의 전국 중학교 기출 문제 및 교과서 완전 분석 후 반영

단어장 및 추가 연습문제 제공

www.taborm.com

주니어 고릴라 영문법 Level 2 | Junior Gorilla Grammar 2

저자 타보름 교재 개발팀

디자인 김경희

발행인 이선미

발행일 개정 4쇄 2022년 3월 1일

발행처 타보름 교육

홈페이지 www.taborm.com

주니어
고릴라 영문법
교재 소개

문법 공부를 위한 문법책이 아닙니다.

1회성 시험만을 위한 문법책이 아닙니다.

그것보다는 조금은 욕심을 냈습니다.

시행착오를 겪기 전에
반복할 수 있게 했습니다.

영어가 싫어지지 않을 만큼만
반복하게 했습니다.

자신감이 붙어 즐길 수 있게 될 만큼만
반복하게 했습니다.

교육 이론만 가지고 만든 교재가 아닙니다.

1년간 수업을 해보고
더하기 빼기를 한 후 나온 교재입니다.

- 타보름 교재 개발팀

타보름 대표 교재
한 눈에 보기

주니어 고릴라 영문법 Level 1,2,3

추천 대상 | 중등부
중등부의 탄탄한 기초와 흥미 유지를 위한
핵심 반복과 영작 연습!

무료 동영상 강의 및 추가 문제 제공
정가 13,500원 (Level 1)
14,200원 (Level 2, 3)

핵꿀잼 리딩 Level 1,2,3

추천 대상 | 중등부
사랑, 공포, 지식, 유머, 심리 테스트까지
독해 욕구 완전 풀가동!

정가 12,000원 (Level 1,2,3)

수능X고등내신 영문법 2400제

추천 대상 | 고등부

문법 기초부터 심화까지 독해에

필수적인 문법만을 반복해서 연습

단원별로 제공되는 수능 기출예문을 통해

실적 감각도 상승!

정가 14,300원

교육부 지정 중고등 영단어 3000

추천 대상 | 성인 및 중고등부

교육부가 지정한 필수 영단어를 포켓북으로!

랜덤 단어 무제한 테스트 생성기

무료제공으로 확실하게 암기한다

무제한 단어 테스트 생성기 무료제공

정가 6,800원

수능x내신 고등 영단어 1만

추천 대상 | 성인 및 고등부

수능, 내신, EBS 연계교재의 빈출 필수 영단어 1만개 포함.

자주 사용되는 순서대로 2,500단어씩 총 4개 파트로 구분.

유사 어원/파생어군 통합 배치하여 암기 작업 최소화.

무제한 단어 테스트 생성기 무료제공

정가 11,200원

unit 3 인칭대명사

인칭		격 수	주격 (주어자리)	소유격 (명사수식)	목적격 (목적어자리)	소유대명사
1인칭		단수	I	my	me	mine
		복수	we	our	us	ours
2인칭		단수	you	your	you	your
		복수	you	your	you	your
3인칭	단 수	남성	he	his	him	h
		여성	she	her	her	
		중성	it	its	it	
		복수	they	their	them	

★ 용어설명
- 1인칭: '나(본인)'를 말한다.
- 2인칭: '너(상대방)'를 말한다.
- 3인칭: '나'와 '너'를 제외한 모든 것을 말한다.

- 단수: 한 개
- 복수: 둘 이상

주어	동사	목적어	해석
I	met	her.	나는 그
She	met	him.	그
He	met	us.	
We	met	them.	
They	met		

se 1

어진 단어에 맞는 인칭대명사

1. John → (you / he / they)

2. Mike and Sue → (she / they /

3. My Friends → (he / she / the

4. Jane's → (she / her / him)

5. My watch → (he / ours / min

6. A book → (it / they / you)

7. I and you → (they / herself /

8. You and me → (them / us / i

Her pencil → (she / her / her

ir money → (we / us / th

step 2
부가 문제를 통한
깨달음 유도

step 1 깔끔하고
잡은 설명

추가 문제 및 단원 종합문제는 홈페이지 및 카페에 다양한 버전으로 다운 받을 수 있습니다.

cise 2 --------------------------

어진 단어를 이용하여 영작하시오.

그녀는 예쁘지 않다. (pretty)

그는 매우 잘 생겼다. (handsome)

그들은 친절하다. (kind)

너는 혼자니? (alone)

나는 집에 있다. (home)

step **4**

여러 단계에 걸친
테스트!

step **3**

이해종결 을 위한
영작!

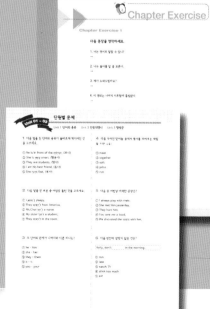

Chapter Exercise

Chapter Exercise 1

다음 문장을 영작하세요.

1. 나는 영어로 말할 수 있니?
→

2. 나는 물어볼 답 을 모른다.
→

3. 제가 노래도청하나요?
→

4. 이 영화는 나에게 기쁨함께 즐겁었다.

단원별 문제

Unit 01 ~ 03   Unit 1 단어의 종류   Unit 2 인칭대명사   Unit 3 형태상

Exercise

Unit Exercise 1

괄호 안에 알맞은 표현을 고르고 해석하세요.

1. He never tells me (what /that) I want to hear from

2. (Whether /If) she can speak Korean is uncertain.

3. (That /Whether) your father is rich or not is not i

4. I wonder (why /what) he can swim well.

5. This is (that /what) he wants to have.

6. She doesn't believe (that /why) I am a liar.

7. I think (that /when) this is a spoon.

8. (What /How) I have lived my life can affect his ch

주니어 고릴라 영문법의 학습 구성

Junior Gorilla Grammar Level 2

주니어 고릴라 영문법 2

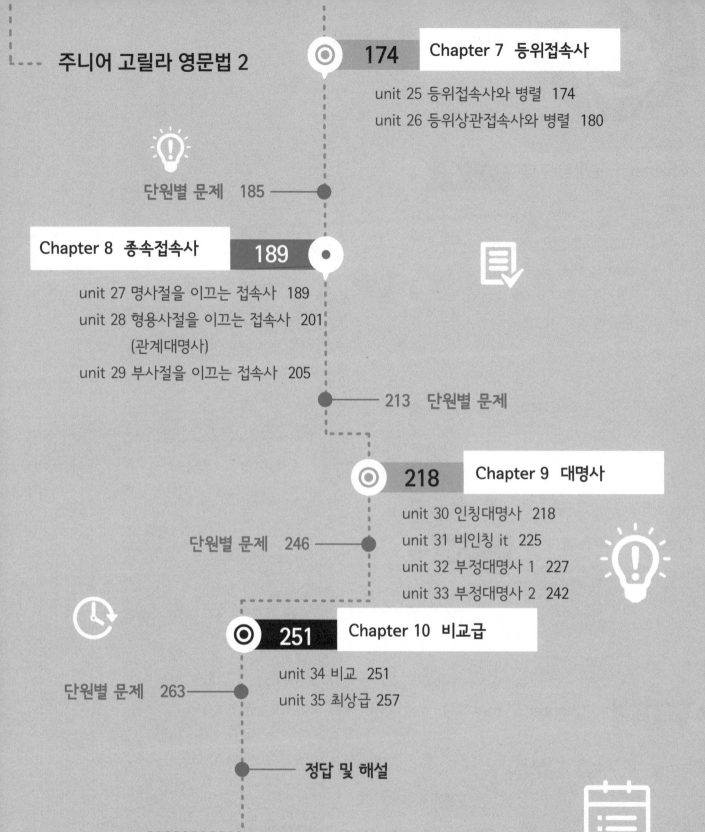

1 문장의 구성
Chapter

Gorilla Grammar

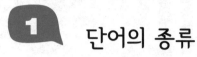

1 단어의 종류

- **(대)명사:** 생물이나 무생물의 이름을 나타내는 말.
  (ex: 주희, 서연, 책상, 도덕, 모래, 물 등)

  - **대명사는 명사를 대신해 쓰는 말이다.**
    (ex: 그, 그녀, 그것, 그들 등)

- **동사:** 주어의 동작이나 상태를 나타내는 말.
  (ex: 자다, 놀다, 공부하다 등)

  - **문장의 형식은 동사에 달려있음** (ex: sleep-1형식, be동사-1,2형식, meet-3형식)
  - **동사로 시제와 태를 나타낸다.** (ex: 잔다, 잤다, 잘 것이다 등)

- **형용사:** 문장에서 명사를 수식하거나 보어 자리에 들어간다.
  (ex: 예쁜, 귀여운, 착한, 경건한 등)
  (활용: 예쁜 주희, 귀여운 서연 등)

- **부사:** 형용사, 동사, 또 다른 부사, 문장전체의 수식을 담당한다.
  (ex: 잘, 너무, 매우, 예쁘게, 귀엽게, 착하게 등)
  (활용: 너무 예쁜, 잘 잔다, 등)

"전치사 + 명사 = 부사"
역시 문장 안에서 수식의 역할만 합니다^^

---- **Exercise 1** --

다음 제시된 단어들의 종류를 하나만 쓰세요.

1. 시계 _____   2. 수영하다 _____

3. 그들의 _____   4. 불쌍한 _____

5. 크게 _____   6. 물 _____

7. 자주 _____   8. 컵 _____

9. 믿음 _____   10. 앉다 _____

---- **Exercise 1-1** --

다음 제시된 단어들의 종류를 하나만 쓰세요.

1. handsome _____   2. often _____

3. do _____   4. watch _____

5. study _____   6. beautiful _____

7. pretty _____   8. our _____

9. TV _____   10. write _____

unit 2 문장의 종류

1 문장의 종류

- 1형식: ^(주인공)주어 + 동사.
  명+은/는/이/가
- 2형식: 주어 + 동사 + 주격 보어.
  (보충어)
- 3형식: 주어 + 동사 + 목적어.
  명/형
- 4형식: 주어 + 동사 + 간접목적어 + 직접목적어.
  ~에게   ~을/를
- 5형식: 주어 + 동사 + 목적어 + 목적 보어.

★ 주어: 문장의 주인공

  보어: 보충어

  ex) 주격보어: 주어를 보충 설명

2 문장의 구성

:문장을 구성하는 단어의 역할을 살펴보자.

- 명사: 주어, 목적어, 보어 역할
- 동사: 동사
- 형용사: 보어, 명사 수식
- 부사: 문장 구성 안 함. 명사를 제외하고 다 수식

  ★ 전치사+명사=부사

unit 3 1형식과 2형식

1형식

:주어와 동사만으로 문장이 성립한다.

일반적인 1형식 동사들
go, come, smile, sleep, sing, die 등

- The birds sing.

  그 새들은 노래한다.

- The leaves fell.

  그 잎사귀들이 떨어졌다.

2형식

:주어, 동사 그리고 주어를 보충해주는 (주격)보어로 구성된다.

a. 2형식 대표 동사: be 동사 (~이다)

- She is smart.

  그녀는 똑똑하다.

- She is a student.

  그녀는 학생이다.

b. 감각동사

: 보통 2형식 동사와는 달리 보어자리에 형용사만이 온다.

감각동사	feel (~하게 느끼다), look (~하게 보이다), sound (~하게 들리다), smell (~한 냄새가 나다), taste (~한 맛이 나다)

- You **look** great.

  너는 멋져 보인다.

- The soup **tastes** salty.

  그 스프는 짠 맛이 난다.

- This perfume **smells** good.

  이 향수는 좋은 냄새가 난다.

- He **felt** hungry.

  그는 배고픈 것을 느꼈다.

- His plan **sounds** perfect.

  그의 계획은 완벽한 것처럼 들린다.

- -

★ 감각동사 뒤에 보어로 명사를 쓰고자할 경우 like와 함께 쓴다.

- At that time, I felt like an idiot.

  그 당시에, 나는 바보가 된 것 같았다.

- I feel ~~like~~ hungry.

  나는 배고프다고 느낀다.

- It sounds like a good plan.

  그것은 좋은 계획처럼 들린다.

- It sounds ~~like~~ great.

  그것은 훌륭한 것처럼 들린다.

---- **Exercise 1** --

다음 문장들은 몇 형식 문장인지 밝히고 해석하세요.

1. A bird flies. (   )

2. She is honest. (   )

3. They felt free. (   )

4. I am busy. (   )

5. They got drunk. (   )

6. She is in the heaven. (   )

7. She is an angel. (   )

8. Tom became a teacher. (   )

9. This milk went bad. (   )

10. I went to church on Sunday. (   )

EXERCISE

다음 문장들이 몇 형식 문장인지 밝히고 해석하세요.

1. The sun set at 6 p.m. today. (   )

2. She seems beautiful among them. (   )

3. The man swam in the pool. (   )

4. My son became a doctor. (   )

5. I tried hard. (   )

6. I don't care about it. (   )

7. Time flies. (   )

8. We are not rich. (   )

9. The leaves turned red and yellow. (   )

10. It gets hot in summer. (   )

---- **Exercise 2** --

다음 문장들을 문법적으로 옳게 고치세요.

1. This cover feels like smooth.

2. She looks a movie star.

3. This shampoo smells like good.

4. That sounds greatly.

5. The stars seem like bright.

---- **Exercise 2-1** --

다음 문장들을 문법적으로 옳게 고치세요.

1. This apple tastes sweetly.

2. The product feels like soft.

3. This car looks like expensive.

4. Some healthy food tastes like bitter.

5. The boy seems like happy.

EXERCISE

---- **Exercise 3** --

다음 주어진 문장을 영작하세요.

1. John은 매일 잔다.

→

2. 시간은 화살처럼 날아간다. (arrow)

→

3. 그녀는 가수처럼 보인다.

→

4. 이 베개는 부드럽게 느껴진다. (pillow)

→

5. 이 빵은 맛있어 보인다.

→

---- **Exercise 3-1** --

다음 주어진 문장을 영작하세요.

1. 나의 엄마는 젊어 보인다.

→

2. 해는 동쪽에서 뜬다. (east)

→

3. 그들은 항상 방안에서 노래한다.

→

4. 의자 밑에 고양이 한 마리가 있다. (There~)

→

5. 봄에는 잎들이 녹색으로 변한다. (leaves)

→

unit 4 3형식과 4형식

1 3형식

a. 3형식 기본 형태: <u>주어 + 동사 + 목적어</u>

b. 3형식 대표동사

meet, like, eat, make, visit, use, clean, open 등

- I like him a lot.
  나는 그를 많이 좋아한다.
- I used his computer.
  나는 그의 컴퓨터를 사용했다.

2 4형식

a. 4형식 기본 형태: <u>주어 + 동사 + 간접목적어 (~에게) + 직접목적어 (을/를)</u>

b. 4형식 대표 동사

give, make, lend, send, show, tell, buy, write, cook 등

- I gave him a present.
  나는 그에게 선물 하나를 주었다.
- She made me a cake.
  그녀는 나에게 케이크 하나를 만들어 주었다.
- They showed him the pictures.
  그들은 그에게 사진들을 보여주었다.

EXERCISE

---- **Exercise 1** --

다음 문장들이 몇 형식 문장인지 밝히고 해석하세요.

1. Terry told me a secret. (   )

2. My boyfriend bought me a bunch of roses. (   )

3. I washed the dishes. (   )

4. We know the truth. (   )

5. They lent me some money. (   )

---- **Exercise 1-1** --

다음 문장들이 몇 형식 문장인지 밝히고 해석하세요.

1. They love me a lot. (   )

2. He threw me a book. (   )

3. The suspect didn't admit his guilt. (   )

4. The host awarded my son a silver medal. (   )

5. My mom dried her hair with a hair dryer. (   )

unit 4 3형식과 4형식

 4형식을 3형식으로 전환

: 4형식 문장을 간접목적어와 직접목적어의 위치를 바꾸고 그 사이에 알맞은 전치사를 넣음으로써 3형식 문장으로 바꿔 쓸 수 있다.

4형식 문장 주어 + 동사 + 간접목적어 + 직접목적어.	
↓	
3형식 문장 주어 + 동사 + 직접목적어 + 전치사 + 간접목적어.	

★ 전치사 고르기

of	ask 등
for	buy, make, get, find, cook, build 등
to	tell, give, lend, send, show, teach, bring 등

• I asked him a personal question.

→ I asked a personal question **of** him.

　　나는 그에게 개인적인 질문 하나를 했다.

• She made me a cake.

→ She made a cake **for** me.

　　그녀는 나에게 케이크 하나를 만들어줬다.

• They showed him the pictures.

→ They showed the pictures **to** him.

　　그들은 그에게 사진들을 보여줬다.

EXERCISE

다음 4형식 문장들을 3형식으로 전환하세요.

1. My girlfriend gave me a present.

→

2. My dad made me a chair.

→

3. His mom cooks him ramen.

→

4. I built my son a small house.

→

5. They bought me something special.

→

6. You showed her your love.

→

7. They sent him a book.

→

---- **Exercise 1-1** --

다음 3형식 문장들을 4형식으로 전환하세요.

1. Lucas bought a bicycle for Jane.

→

2. I asked a favor of you.

→

3. We found a job for you.

→

4. John sent a letter to his mom.

→

5. The waiter brought an onion soup to me.

→

6. My mom gave some cookies to me.

→

---- Exercise 2 --

다음 주어진 문장을 영작하세요.

1. 나는 그에게 지갑을 사줬다. (a wallet)

→

2. 나는 선생님께 질문을 하나 했다. (a question)

→

3. 그는 나에게 그 박스를 보냈다. (the box)

→

4. 나는 그의 가난을 이해한다. (poverty)

→

5. 나는 점심 식사를 했다. (have)

→

---- Exercise 2-1 --

다음 주어진 문장을 영작하세요.

1. 나에게 소금을 건네주세요. (pass)

→

2. 나는 그 책을 읽었다.

→

3. Jane은 그들에게 비밀을 말했다. (a secret)

→

4. 나는 선물을 원한다. (a present)

→

5. 그녀는 나에게 시계를 빌려줬다. (a watch)

→

unit 5   5형식

1 5형식 기본

a. 5형식 기본 형태: 주어 + 동사 + 목적어 + 목적격보어.

  • 목적격보어는 목적어를 보충 설명한다.

b. 5형식 대표동사

make, find, think, elect 등

• I made him a teacher.

  나는 그를 선생님으로 만들었다. (그가 선생님)

• I consider her smart.

  나는 그녀가 똑똑하다고 생각한다. (그녀가 똑똑)

EXERCISE

괄호 안에서 올바른 문장의 형식을 선택하고 해석하세요.

1. I found his advice useless. (4형식 / 5형식)

2. He made his son a doctor. (4형식 / 5형식)

3. They make me crazy. (4형식 / 5형식)

4. He bought me dinner yesterday. (4형식 / 5형식)

5. My mom made me a cake. (4형식 / 5형식)

6. They elected him chairman. (4형식 / 5형식)

7. The teacher bought me a textbook. (4형식 / 5형식)

8. He asked her a question. (4형식 / 5형식)

---- **Exercise 1-1** --

괄호 안에서 올바른 문장의 형식을 선택하고 해석하세요.

1. My dad gave me his watch. (4형식 / 5형식)

2. She made him a vet. (4형식 / 5형식)

3. We named her Jane. (4형식 / 5형식)

4. I often show him something funny. (4형식 / 5형식)

5. Susan found the book difficult. (4형식 / 5형식)

6. His father will leave him a large fortune. (4형식 / 5형식)

7. Tom made me a nice sandwich. (4형식 / 5형식)

8. We built him a tall building. (4형식 / 5형식)

unit 5 5형식

2 5형식 응용

a. 사역동사 (make, have, let): <u>주어 + 동사 + 목적어 + 동사원형</u>

• I let my son do the dishes.

　나는 내 아들이 설거지를 하게했다.

• She made him clean her house.

　그녀는 그가 그녀의 집을 청소하게 했다.

b. 지각동사 (hear, feel, watch, see 등): <u>주어 + 동사 + 목적어 + 동사원형 /~ing</u>

• I heard her crying. (o)

• I heard her cry. (o)

　나는 그녀가 우는 것을 들었다.

c. 그 밖의 동사 (want, persuade, expect 등): <u>주어 + 동사 + 목적어 + to 동사원형</u>

• I want you to study hard.

　나는 네가 공부를 열심히 하기를 원한다.

• He persuaded me to buy the junk.

　그는 내가 그 쓰레기를 사도록 설득했다.

★ 다수의 예외가 있지만 준사역 help는 꼭 기억하자.

→ 주어+ help + 목적어 + (to)동사원형.

• She helped me (to) escape from him.

　그녀는 내가 그로부터 탈출하는 것을 도왔다.

다음 주어진 문장들을 해석하세요.

1. The teacher asked me to tell the secret.

→

2. I told her to take the test.

→

3. They want me to join the club.

→

4. People in the building heard someone screaming at a girl.

→

5. I persuaded him to meet her.

→

6. They smelled something burning in the office.

→

---- **Exercise 1-1** --

다음 주어진 문장들을 해석하세요.

1. People keep the accident a secret.

→

2. They heard birds singing in the tree.

→

3. A student asked the teacher not to give him homework.

→

4. They want me to drive this car.

→

5. He had his roommate clean the room.

→

---- **Exercise 2** --

다음 문장들을 문법적으로 옳게 고치세요.

1. I expect him calling me soon.

2. I will make Tom went to the library.

3. I saw her to sing a song.

4. I told him come here.

5. I'd like her go to swim with us.

6. May I ask you lending me some books?

7. I saw her to dancing.

8. She made people to laugh continuously.

9. I want you finish this work first.

10. She heard someone to shouting at her.

EXERCISE

다음 문장을 문법적으로 옳게 고치세요.

1. I expect John finish the project in time.

2. We heard her to play the piano.

3. They saw me to laugh loudly.

4. They had me did it at once.

5. Let him to introduce himself.

6. Jane asks Tom clean her room.

7. I felt someone to hitting me.

8. I told Jane wash the dishes.

9. I heard the phone rang.

10. We asked the philosopher teach us how to live a happy life.

---- **Exercise 3** ---

다음 문장들을 5형식 문장으로 영작하세요.

1. 그녀는 그녀의 개가 빨리 달리는 것을 보았다.

→ She watched _____ .

2. 나는 그들이 집에서 노래 부르는 것을 들었다.

→ I heard _____ .

3. 나는 네가 한국어 공부하는 것을 도와주겠다.

→ I will help _____ .

4. 그는 그 자신을 천재라고 불렀다.

→ He called _____ .

5. John은 그 영화가 매력적이었다는 것을 알았다. (attractive)

→ John found _____ .

6. David는 그녀에게 설거지를 하라고 말했다.

→ David told _____ .

7. 의장의 직권으로 나는 너에게 이 방에서 퇴장할 것을 명한다. (leave)

→ On my authority as chairman, I order _____ .

8. 그는 그의 몸 안에서 분노가 치밀어 오르는 것을 느꼈다. (the anger / rise)

→ He felt _____ .

9. 이 가방은 내가 무거운 책들을 옮길 수 있게 도와준다. (carry)

→ This bag helps _____ .

EXERCISE

다음 문장들을 5형식 문장으로 영작하세요.

1. 나의 엄마는 내가 내 방을 청소하게 했다.

→ My mom made _____ .

2. 그들은 내가 그 팀에 가입하기를 원한다. (join)

→ They want _____ .

3. 의사는 그녀에게 금연할 것을 권유했다. (quit)

→ The doctor advised _____ .

4. 나는 그 생각이 매우 좋다고 간주했다.

→ I considered _____ .

5. 나는 그가 Mac을 설득하도록 도왔다. (persuade)

→ I helped _____ .

6. 나는 맥주를 마시고 있는 소년을 보았다. (beer)

→ I saw _____ .

7. John은 새들이 평화롭게 노래하는 것을 들었다.

→ John heard _____ .

8. 나는 그가 가도록하지 않을 것이다.

→ I will never let _____ .

Exercise 1

다음 문장들이 몇 형식 문장인지 밝히고 해석하세요.

1. They watched a movie. (   )

2. She looks upset. (   )

3. The fairy disappeared. (   )

4. You look fantastic. (   )

5. They are good friends. (   )

6. I bought my wife a new ring. (   )

7. I don't believe Sally to be a liar. (   )

8. Can I use your laptop? (   )

9. I found her a nice house. (   )

10. I found her nice house. (   )

Exercise 1-1

다음 문장들이 몇 형식 문장인지 밝히고 해석하세요.

1. I attended the conference. (   )

2. We call her Pretty. (   )

3. This chocolate tastes bad. (   )

4. He fell on his knees. (   )

5. Nothing can prevent me from doing my duty. (   )

6. The children like puppies. (   )

7. I consider him dumb. (   )

8. Her plan sounds wonderful. (   )

9. Can you teach me Spanish 3 times a week? (   )

10. Our dream came true in many respects. (   )

단원 결합문제

Unit 1-5

Exercise 1-2

다음 문장들이 몇 형식 문장인지 밝히고 해석하세요.

1. The stranger was very kind. (   )

2. Lots of people are in the building. (   )

3. Many reporters gathered around. (   )

4. The house remains unchanged. (   )

5. The situation is hardly understandable. (   )

6. This clock doesn't work at all. (   )

7. She grew some plants. (   )

8. She felt unpleasant with him. (   )

9. I often tell a lie to him. (   )

10. Her excuse made me angry. (   )

unit 6 감탄문

1   What + a + 형용사 + 명사 (+ 주어 + 동사)!

- What a beautiful house (it is)!

  그것은 정말 아름다운 집이구나!

- What a pretty girl (she is)!

  그녀는 정말 예쁜 소녀구나!

★ 명사가 복수형일 때 'a'를 쓰는 실수를 하지 않도록 조심
- What lovely daughters (you have)!

  너는 정말 사랑스러운 딸들이 있구나!

2   How + 형용사 /부사 (+ 주어 + 동사)!

- How small (the world is)!

  세상은 참 작구나!

- How hot (the weather is)!

  날씨가 정말 덥구나!

---- **Exercise 1** --

다음 문장들을 How로 시작하는 감탄문으로 바꾸세요.

1. She is so kind.

→

2. Tom is so tall.

→

3. The car is so expensive.

→

4. John is so smart.

→

5. Jane is very rich.

→

EXERCISE

다음 문장을 What으로 시작하는 감탄문으로 바꾸세요.

1. He is a famous actor.

→

2. She bought a luxury bag.

→

3. You did a wonderful thing.

→

4. We are very good friends.

→

5. Sean built a gorgeous house.

→

Unit Exercise

Chapter 1 문장의 종류

01 다음 밑줄 친 부분의 문장 성분이 나머지 넷과 다른 것은?

① I will have lunch <u>at home</u>.
② He bought some food <u>for me</u>.
③ I opened the window <u>slowly</u>.
④ I found him <u>friendly</u>.
⑤ I borrowed some money <u>from her</u>.

02 다음 중 밑줄 친 부분이 어법상 틀린 것은?

① She <u>looked very happy</u>.
② He <u>looked at</u> the score board.
③ The boy <u>looked sadly</u>.
④ I was <u>looking for</u> my pen.
⑤ She <u>looks like</u> a cartoon character.

03 다음 중 어법상 맞는 문장은?

① It looks excitingly.
② This milk tastes weirdly.
③ These socks feel softly.
④ She looks lovely today.
⑤ The tree smells wonderfully.

04 다음 빈칸에 들어갈 말로 알맞지 <u>않은</u> 것은?

He_____some pictures of France to me.

① sent
② handed
③ got
④ showed
⑤ passed

05 다음 빈칸에 공통으로 들어갈 전치사를 적으세요.

• She gave a comic book_____me.
• Jane teaches Korean_____us.

06 다음 중 밑줄 친 부분의 의미가 나머지 넷과 다른 것은?

① He <u>had</u> a computer in his room.
② He <u>had</u> his brother read the book.
③ He <u>had</u> the student clean the classroom.
④ He <u>had</u> his wife prepare dinner for them.
⑤ He <u>had</u> us put away all the garbage.

07 다음 빈칸에 들어갈 말로 알맞은 것은?

> Mr. Harrison doesn't want me
> _____with the trouble makers.

① to hung out
② to hang out
③ hang out
④ hung out
⑤ to hangs out

08 다음 중 문장의 형식이 나머지와 다른 하나를 고르세요.

① Your hands feel warm.
② You looked upset this morning.
③ This chicken soup smells good.
④ Miss Bennet made a dress for me.
⑤ The birds' song always sounds sweet.

09 다음 빈칸에 들어갈 말로 알맞은 것은?

> My cousin_____me her beautiful blue dress.

① had
② turned
③ wanted
④ lent
⑤ borrowed

10 다음 주어진 문장들이 몇 형식인지 맞추고 해석 하세요.

(1) She appeared suddenly.

(2) She appears weak.

11 다음 중 밑줄 친 부분의 쓰임이 나머지 넷과 다른 것은?

① He will buy <u>a cell phone</u>.
② He didn't say <u>anything</u> to me.
③ They planned <u>a wonderful party</u>.
④ Do you remember <u>our first date</u>?
⑤ I will call you <u>my little princess</u>.

12 다음 빈칸에 들어갈 말로 알맞지 않은 것은?

> The accessory looks_____. I'll buy it.

① cheap
② pretty
③ cutely
④ lovely
⑤ beautiful

13 다음 빈칸에 들어갈 말로 바르게 짝 지어진 것은?

> • We heard the man_____a speech.
> • We saw her_____downstairs.

① make - coming
② make - to come
③ making - to come
④ to make - coming
⑤ to make - come

[14-15] 다음 문장을 감탄문으로 고쳐 쓸 때 빈칸에 알맞은 말을 쓰세요.

14. The movie is really interesting.

→ _____ _____the movie is!

15. You have a very nice car.

→ _____ _____ _____car you have!

16 다음 빈칸에 들어갈 말로 알맞지 <u>않은</u> 것은?

> The sound of raindrops_____me relax.

① helps
② has
③ gets
④ makes
⑤ lets

17 다음 글의 밑줄 친 부분 중 어법상 <u>틀린</u> 것은?

> A: <u>You're late again</u>!
>   ①
> B: I'm sorry, sir. My mother <u>made me to</u>
>   <u>clean</u> my room <u>before going</u> out.
>   ②   ③
>   I <u>had no choice</u>.
>   ④
> A: Even so, <u>be on time</u>!
>   ⑤

18 다음 중 어법상 <u>틀린</u> 것은?

① My mother had me go to sleep early.
② I want you take a chance.
③ Jane made her husband help me.
④ My parents let me go to the party.
⑤ My grandmother made me a dress.

19 다음 중 밑줄 친 부분의 성격이 나머지와 <u>다른</u> 하나는?

① Kevin sent her family <u>the postcards</u>.
② The boy looked <u>embarrassed</u> after giving the wrong answer.
③ The dishes smelled good but tasted <u>awful</u>.
④ The weather is <u>very hot</u> here in Hawaii.
⑤ Their children became <u>great musicians</u>.

20 다음 빈칸에 들어갈 말로 알맞지 <u>않은</u> 것은?

> Jack told us that he made a perfect plan for our camping, but the plan didn't sound_____.

① nice
② interesting
③ great
④ excellently
⑤ perfect

21 다음 문장을 5형식 문장으로 고쳐 쓰세요.

> I found that the bag is heavy.
>
> → _____

22 다음 중 문장의 형식이 나머지와 <u>다른</u> 하나는?

① I made my daughter a paper house.
② I gave him some notice.
③ I will find your lost dog.
④ Did you buy your son a car?
⑤ He showed me a portrait of his girlfriend.

23 다음 빈칸에 들어갈 단어가 <u>다른</u> 하나는?

① _____ a kind boy he is!
② _____ beautiful the scenery is!
③ _____ cute cats they are!
④ _____ a sad story!
⑤ _____ a small dog!

[**24-25**] 다음 빈칸에 주어진 단어의 형태를 필요하면 바꿔서 써넣으세요.

24 I heard him_____the guitar. (play)

25 I expected them_____me. (visit)

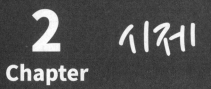

2 시제

Chapter

Gorilla Grammar

unit 7 현재와 현재진행

: 현재진행형의 기본형은 am/are/is +ing 이며, 지금 현재 진행되고 있는 일을 나타내고자 할 때 쓴다.

 ## 동사의 -ing형 만들기

대부분의 동사	-ing	go - going do - doing sell - selling study - studying
자음 + -e로 끝나는 동사	e를 빼고 -ing	make - making give - giving
-ie로 끝나는 동사	ie를 y로 바꾸고 -ing	lie - lying die - dying
단모음 + 단자음 으로 끝나는 동사	마지막 자음을 한 번 더 쓰고 -ing	hit - hitting cut - cutting run - running stop - stopping

• The students are playing soccer now.

그 학생들은 지금 축구를 하고 있는 중이다.

• I am studying English now.

나는 지금 영어를 공부하고 있는 중이다.

• She is running toward the building now.

그녀는 지금 빌딩을 향해 달려가고 있는 중이다.

---- **Exercise 1** --

다음 주어진 동사들의 +ing를 쓰세요.

1. eat	_____	2. make	_____
3. lay	_____	4. buy	_____
5. sleep	_____	6. carry	_____
7. sell	_____	8. understand	_____
9. have	_____	10. jog	_____
11. borrow	_____	12. tell	_____
13. fight	_____	14. listen	_____

---- **Exercise 1-1** --

다음 주어진 동사들의 +ing를 쓰세요.

1. dream	_____	2. love	_____
3. put	_____	4. lose	_____
5. live	_____	6. shut	_____
7. lend	_____	8. hear	_____
9. swim	_____	10. walk	_____
11. drink	_____	12. sing	_____
13. shop	_____	14. pass	_____

EXERCISE

다음 문장을 현재 진행형으로 바꾸세요.

1. She tells the story to us.

→

2. I buy some shirts.

→

3. Bob speaks loudly.

→

4. The birds sing a song.

→

5. John falls asleep.

→

6. She shops in the department store.

→

7. It rains.

→

8. They study math.

→

9. He dances on the floor.

→

10. She plays the guitar.

→

---- **Exercise 2-1** --

다음 문장을 현재시제로 바꾸세요.

1. We are buying some food.

→

2. They are running fast.

→

3. Sally is listening to the music.

→

4. I am swimming in the ocean.

→

5. Sean is driving to his home.

→

6. We are singing a song.

→

7. She is laughing loudly.

→

8. He is spending too much money.

→

9. The ring is shining in the dark.

→

10. They are changing colors.

→

unit 7 현재와 현재진행

2 현재와 현재진행형의 비교

현재	현재의 사실, 상태, 습관, 반복적 행위를 나타낼 때
현재진행	현재 행해지고 있는 동작의 연속을 나타낸다.

a. He plays the piano (every Sunday).

그는 피아노를 연주한다. (매주 일요일마다)

b. He is playing the piano (now).

그는 지금 피아노를 연주하고 있는 중이다. (지금)

- -

★ ①은 지금 당장 피아노를 연주하고 있는 것이 아니라 He에 대한 일종의 배경 설명이 된다.

즉, 그는 매주 일요일마다 피아노를 치는 사람이라는 것이다.

반면에 ②은 지금 당장 피아노를 치는 일에 주력하고 있다는 것을 암시한다.

a. He is honest. (usually)

그는 정직하다. (주로)

b. He is being honest. (temporarily)

그는 정직하게 행동하고 있다. (일시적으로)

- -

★ ①에서 그는 보통 정직한 사람이라는 뜻이고, ②에서 그는 평소에는 아닐지라도 지금
순간만큼은 정직하게 행동하고 있는 집중도를 나타낸다.

---- **Exercise 1** --

다음 괄호 안에서 적절한 표현을 고르세요.

1. She (plays /is playing) the violin every weekend.

2. Unicorns actually (exist / are existing).

3. They (don't like / aren't liking) her.

4. She (plays / is playing) soccer now.

5. He (looks / is looking) sad.

6. Students (go / is going) to school every day.

7. She (has / is having) a cat.

8. The pot (boils / is boiling) now.

9. Water (boils / is boiling) at 100℃.

10. They (always make / are always making) me happy.

EXERCISE

다음 괄호 안에서 적절한 표현을 고르세요.

1. They sometimes (fight /are fighting) each other.

2. The creature (is /is being) alive in the lake.

3. She (lives / is living) in Tokyo.

4. He never (tells / is telling) a lie.

5. He (tells /is telling) a lie for now to avoid being grounded.

6. The perfume (smells /is smelling) like a rose.

7. She often (cries /is crying) hard.

8. He (studies /is studying) every day.

9. He (studies /is studying) English now.

10. They (give /are giving) me a bouquet of flowers every Monday.

---- **Exercise 2** --

다음 문장을 영작 하세요.

1. 나는 지금 낮잠을 자고 있다. (take a nap)

→

2. 나는 매일 낮잠을 잔다.

→

3. 우리는 일요일 아침마다 교회에 간다.

→

4. Poly는 항상 아침에 일찍 일어난다.

→

5. 태양은 동쪽에서 뜬다. (rise)

→

---- **Exercise 2-1** --

다음 문장을 영작 하세요.

1. 나는 집에서 열심히 공부하고 있다.

→

2. 나는 매일 열심히 공부한다.

→

3. 우리는 축구를 하고 있다.

→

4. 우리는 일요일마다 축구한다.

→

5. 그들은 저녁을 먹고 있다. (have)

→

unit 8 과거와 과거진행

과거

: 과거의 사실을 단순히 서술할 때 쓴다. 현재까지 이어지지 않는다.

- • I slept well yesterday.

  나는 어제 잘 잤다.
- • I was silly.

  나는 어리석었다.

a. 일반 동사의 과거형 만들기 (규칙)

동사의 종류	만드는 방법	예시
대부분의 동사 + -e 로 끝나는 동사	동사원형 + (e)d를 붙인다.	worked, finished, helped, liked, danced,..
자음+y 로 끝나는 동사	y를 i로 바꾸고, -ed를 붙인다.	try → tried, study → studied
모음+y 로 끝나는 동사	그대로 -ed를 붙인다.	enjoyed, stayed,…
단모음+단자음 으로 끝나는 1음절 동사	자음을 한 번 더 쓰고 -ed를 붙인다.	stopped, planned,…

unit 8 과거와 과거진행

b. 일반 동사의 과거형 만들기 (불규칙)

기본형	과거형	의미	기본형	과거형	의미
be	was /were	이다, 있다	leave	left	떠나다, 남다
become	became	되다	lend	lent	빌려주다
begin	began	시작하다	let	let	하게 하다
break	broke	깨뜨리다	lose	lost	잃다
bring	brought	가져오다	make	made	만들다
build	built	짓다	meet	met	만나다
buy	bought	사다	pay	paid	지불하다
catch	caught	잡다	put	put	두다
choose	chose	선택하다	quit	quit	그만두다
come	came	오다	read	read	읽다
cost	cost	비용이 들다	rise	rose	뜨다
cut	cut	자르다	run	ran	달리다
do	did	하다	say	said	말하다
draw	drew	그리다	see	saw	보다
drink	drank	마시다	sell	sold	팔다
drive	drove	운전하다	send	sent	보내다
eat	ate	먹다	show	showed	보여주다
fall	fell	떨어지다	sing	sang	노래하다
feel	felt	느끼다	sit	sat	앉다
find	found	발견하다	sleep	slept	자다
forget	forgot	잊다	speak	spoke	말하다
get	got	얻다	spend	spent	소비하다
give	gave	주다	stand	stood	서다
go	went	가다	steal	stole	훔치다
grow	grew	자라다	take	took	취하다
have	had	가지다	teach	taught	가르치다
hear	heard	듣다	tell	told	말하다
hold	held	쥐다, 열다	think	thought	생각하다
hurt	hurt	상처 내다	understand	understood	이해하다
know	knew	알다	win	won	이기다

EXERCISE

---- **Exercise 1** --

다음 주어진 동사들의 과거형을 쓰세요.

1. rob _____   2. agree _____

3. marry _____   4. hope _____

5. love _____   6. carry _____

7. clean _____   8. plan _____

9. hurry _____   10. offer _____

11. call _____   12. die _____

13. enjoy _____   14. end _____

---- **Exercise 1-1** --

다음 주어진 단어들의 과거형을 쓰세요.

1. stop _____   2. climb _____

3. beg _____   4. talk _____

5. close _____   6. change _____

7. study _____   8. fly _____

9. drop _____   10. admit _____

11. occur _____   12. fry _____

13. play _____   14. turn _____

unit 8 과거와 과거진행

2 과거진행

: 과거 한 시점에 동작의 연속을 표현할 때 사용한다.

과거진행 기본형태
was /were + 동사ing.

- I was crying (when he told the story).

  나는 울고 있는 중이었다. (그가 이야기를 할 때).

- She was yelling at me (when I played a computer game).

  그녀는 나에게 고함을 지르고 있었다. (내가 컴퓨터게임을 할 때)

EXERCISE

다음 주어진 문장을 과거 진행형으로 바꾸세요.

1. I had lunch.

→

2. I took a bath.

→

3. I called you.

→

4. She studied hard.

→

5. We went to the movies.

→

6. He read a novel.

→

7. I sang a song in the concert hall.

→

8. She cut the paper into stars.

→

9. He stole the bread.

→

10. I drew the picture.

→

---- **Exercise 1-1** ---

다음 주어진 문장을 단순과거형으로 바꾸세요.

1. My dad was washing the dishes.

→

2. We were having dinner.

→

3. They were running away from home.

→

4. I was taking a shower.

→

5. She was going for a swim.

→

6. He was spreading the rumor.

→

7. I was clicking the button.

→

8. We were fighting with the bullies.

→

9. He was kicking the boxes.

→

10. They were driving along the new highway.

→

---- **Exercise 2** --

다음 주어진 문장을 참고해서 빈칸을 채우세요.

1. 그가 나의 방에 들어왔을 때, 나는 자고 있었다.

→ When he entered my room, _____.

2. 나는 어제 술 취했을 때, 말을 너무 많이 하고 있었다. (talk)

→ _____ when I was drunk.

3. 네가 그 컴퓨터 게임하는 동안 나는 그 리포트를 끝냈다.

→ While _____, I finished the report.

4. 내가 일하고 있는 동안, 그는 나를 귀찮게 했다. (bother)

→ _____ while I was working.

5. 나는 내가 마라톤을 하고 있는 동안 행복을 느꼈다. (run a marathon)

→ I felt happy while _____.

---- **Exercise 3** ---

다음 문장을 영작하세요.

1. 나는 빗속을 걷고 있었다. (in the rain)

→

2. 그가 돌아왔을 때, 밖에 비가 많이 내리고 있었다. (outside)

→

3. 내가 수영장에서 수영하고 있을 때, 그 열쇠를 잃어버렸다. (in the pool)

→

4. 내가 요리를 하고 있을 때, 누군가가 침입했다. (break in)

→

5. 그녀는 옆구리에 가방을 끼고 있었다. (carry, under one's arm)

→

6. 그녀는 선풍기 앞에서 그녀의 머리를 말렸다. (in front of the fan)

→

7. 그들은 어제 나의 집에서 피자를 먹었다.

→

---- **Exercise 3-1** --

다음 문장을 영작하세요.

1. 우리는 학교로 걸어갔다.

→

2. 그는 그의 친구들과 축구를 했다.

→

3. 나는 네가 전화했을 때 자고 있었다.

→

4. Jane은 거실에서 TV를 보고 있었다. (living room)

→

5. 우리는 영어를 열심히 공부했다.

→

6. 그들은 설거지를 하고 있었다.

→

7. Tom은 내가 들어왔을 때 노래를 부르고 있었다.

→

unit 9 미래

1 미래를 나타내는 조동사 will

: 미래를 표현하고자 할 때는 조동사 'will'을 사용한다. may와 같은 다른 조동사와 함께 쓰고자
할 때는 'will' 대신에 'be going to' 동사원형을 쓸 수 있다.

- • I will be a doctor.
  나는 의사가 될 것이다.

- • She will find the treasure someday.
  그녀는 언젠가 그 보물을 발견할 것이다.

- • She will may help thousands of people. (x)
- • She may be going to help thousands of people. (o)
  그녀는 아마도 수천 명의 사람들을 도울 것이다.

- -

★ 부정문

- • I will not be a doctor. (= I won't be a doctor.)
  나는 의사가 되지 않을 것이다.

2 be going to 동사원형

: 또한 'be going to v'는 'will'보다 좀 더 예정된 미래에 사용한다.

- • I'm going to spend this weekend solving a riddle.
  나는 수수께끼를 풀면서 이번 주말을 보낼 예정이다.

- • She is going to go to sleep early tonight.
  그녀는 오늘 밤 일찍 잘 예정이다.

EXERCISE

---- **Exercise 1** --

다음 문장을 보기와 같이 바꾸세요.

> 보기
>
> I will call you soon.
> → I am going to call you soon.

1. She will come again.

→

2. He will ask for his friend.

→

3. I will eat later.

→

4. We'll go to the movies tonight.

→

5. John will be an athlete.

→

6. Sooner or later, you will agree with me.

→

---- **Exercice 1-1** --

다음 문장을 보기와 같이 바꾸세요.

보기
I am going to hit you. → I will hit you.

1. They are going to join the club.

→

2. We are going to study in a group.

→

3. He is going to call me tomorrow.

→

4. I am going to go swimming tonight.

→

5. Are you going to be a teacher?

→

6. Everything is going to fall into place.

→

EXERCISE

---- **Exercise 2** ---

다음 주어진 문장을 영작하세요.

1. 나는 이 회사에서 일할 것이다. (this company)

→

2. 그녀는 나에게 전화할 것이다.

→

3. 우리는 같이 저녁을 먹을 것이다.

→

4. Tom은 내일 학교에 가지 않을 것이다.

→

5. 내일은 비가 올 것이다.

→

---- **Exercise 2-1** ---

다음 주어진 문장을 영작하세요.

1. 나는 해외로 나갈 것이다. (go abroad)

→

2. 그녀는 그녀의 집을 팔 것이다. (sell)

→

3. 그들은 차를 빌릴 것이다. (rent)

→

4. 그는 축구 선수가 될 것이다.

→

5. 나는 너에게 다시는 전화하지 않을 것이다. (again)

→

unit 10 현재완료

: 현재완료는 기본적으로 과거부터 시작해서 현재까지 영향을 미치고 있음을 표현하고자 할 때 쓰며, 언제부터 시작됐는지를 보통 밝혀주기 때문에 since (~이래로)나 for (~동안)이 현재완료가 쓰인 문장에 자주 등장한다.

현재완료 기본형태	has /have + 과거분사 (p.p.)

- She **has had** a problem with making friends since she was young.

  그녀는 어렸을 때 이래로 친구사귀는 데 문제가 있어오고 있다.

- He **has taken** part in the organization for 3 years.

  그는 그 조직에 삼년 동안 참여해오고 있다.

- -

★ 부정문 만들 땐 has나 have 뒤에 not이나 never를 붙인다.

- I have never had a cat.

  나는 고양이를 길러 본적이 없다.

- I have not lived in Busan.

  나는 부산에 살아보지 않았다.

★ have/has not의 축약형: haven't/hasn't.

- I haven't lived in Busan.

  나는 부산에 살아보지 않았다.

- She hasn't lived in Busan.

  그녀는 부산에 살아보지 않았다.

★ 의문문 만들 땐 has나 have를 문장 맨 앞으로 꺼낸다.

- Have **you ever** lived in Busan?

  부산에 살아 본 적이 있니?

unit 10 현재완료

  과거분사 형태 만들기

a. 과거분사(p.p.) 만들기 (규칙): 대부분의 동사는 과거형과 과거분사형이 동일하다.

동사의 종류	만드는 방법	예시
대부분의 동사, -e로 끝나는 동사	동사원형 + (e)d를 붙인다.	worked, finished, helped, liked, danced …
자음+y 로 끝나는 동사	y를 i로 바꾸고, -ed를 붙인다.	try → tried, study → studied
모음+y 로 끝나는 동사	그대로 -ed를 붙인다.	enjoyed, stayed …
단모음+단자음 으로 끝나는 1음절 동사	자음을 한 번 더 쓰고 -ed를 붙인다.	stopped, planned …

- examples

기본형	과거형	과거분사 (p.p.)
work	worked	worked
try	tried	tried
enjoy	enjoyed	enjoyed
stop	stopped	stopped

unit 10 현재완료

b. 과거분사(p.p.) 만들기 (불규칙)

기본형	과거형	과거분사 (p.p.)	기본형	과거형	과거분사 (p.p.)
be	was /were	**been**	leave	left	**left**
become	became	**become**	lend	lent	**lent**
begin	began	**begun**	let	let	**let**
break	broke	**broken**	lose	lost	**lost**
bring	brought	**brought**	make	made	**made**
build	built	**built**	meet	met	**met**
buy	bought	**bought**	pay	paid	**paid**
catch	caught	**caught**	put	put	**put**
choose	chose	**chosen**	quit	quit	**quit**
come	came	**come**	read	read	**read**
cost	cost	**cost**	rise	rose	**risen**
cut	cut	**cut**	run	ran	**run**
do	did	**done**	say	said	**said**
draw	drew	**drawn**	see	saw	**seen**
drink	drank	**drunk**	sell	sold	**sold**
drive	drove	**driven**	send	sent	**sent**
eat	ate	**eaten**	show	showed	**showed /shown**
fall	fell	**fallen**	sing	sang	**sung**
feel	felt	**felt**	sit	sat	**sat**
find	found	**found**	sleep	slept	**slept**
forget	forgot	**forgotten**	speak	spoke	**spoken**
get	got	**got /gotten**	spend	spent	**spent**
give	gave	**given**	stand	stood	**stood**
go	went	**gone**	steal	stole	**stolen**
grow	grew	**grown**	take	took	**taken**
have	had	**had**	teach	taught	**taught**
hear	heard	**heard**	tell	told	**told**
hold	held	**held**	think	thought	**thought**
hurt	hurt	**hurt**	understand	understood	**understood**
know	knew	**known**	win	won	**won**

EXERCISE

---- **Exercise 1** --

다음 주어진 단어들의 과거분사형을 쓰세요.

1. rob	_____	2. agree	_____
3. marry	_____	4. hope	_____
5. love	_____	6. change	_____
7. study	_____	8. fly	_____
9. drop	_____	10. admit	_____
11. occur	_____	12. fry	_____
13. play	_____	14. turn	_____

---- **Exercise 1-1** --

다음 주어진 단어들의 과거분사형을 쓰세요.

1. stop	_____	2. climb	_____
3. beg	_____	4. talk	_____
5. close	_____	6. carry	_____
7. clean	_____	8. plan	_____
9. hurry	_____	10. offer	_____
11. call	_____	12. die	_____
13. enjoy	_____	14. end	_____

---- **Exercise 2** --

다음 문장을 현재완료형 문장으로 바꾸세요.

1. I work in this company.

→

2. Jane doesn't sleep.

→

3. I see a movie.

→

4. She went to Japan.

→

5. They live in Korea.

→

6. Five years passed.

→

7. This program invites you to Busan.

→

8. We studied together since we were very young.

→

9. We kept in touch with each other for a long time.

→

10. She drove to Incheon.

→

EXERCISE

다음 문장을 현재완료형 문장으로 바꾸세요.

1. I clean my room.

→

2. My mom didn't cook dinner for us.

→

3. He went to the park.

→

4. The bus already left.

→

5. We don't know each other.

→

6. She helped someone twice in her life.

→

7. Jane doesn't do volunteer work.

→

8. The milk already went bad.

→

9. The task isn't stressful for me.

→

10. We had dinner together.

→

2 현재완료의 용법

: 현재완료는 과거 한 시점에서 지금까지 영향을 미친다는 것을 기본으로 4가지의 용법을 가진다.

a. 계속적 용법: 가장 기본적인 용법이며, 앞서 소개한대로 과거의 한 시점에서 시작해서 현재까지 영향을 미칠 때 쓴다.

- He has done his best for a long time.

  그는 오랫동안 최선을 다해오고 있다.

- She has taken pictures of animals since 2013.

  그녀는 2013년 이래로 동물들의 사진을 찍어오고 있다.

b. 경험적 용법: 경험을 말할 때 쓰며, '~한 적이 있다'로 해석한다.

- I have shown my fear to him once.

  나는 그에게 나의 두려움을 한번 보인 적이 있다.

- Have you ever raised an iguana?

  너는 이구아나를 키워본 적이 있니?

★ 참고: • have(has) been: 가본 적이 있다

　　　　• have(has) gone: 가버리고 없다

c. 완료적 용법: 이미 완료가 된 사건을 강조하고자 할 때 쓴다.

- I have already solved the problem without him.

  나는 그 없이 그 문제를 이미 해결했다.

- She has just joined the club.

  그녀는 막 그 동아리에 참여했다.

d. 결과적 용법: 과거에 종료된 일의 결과가 현재까지 영향을 미칠 때 사용한다.

- She has lost the guide book, so she has to do it by herself.

  그녀는 안내 책을 잃어버렸다, 그래서 그녀는 그것을 혼자서 해야만 한다.

- I have bought a pen, so I don't need to memorize what I have to remember.

  나는 펜 하나를 샀다, 그래서 나는 내가 기억해야만 하는 것을 암기할 필요가 없다.

---- **Exercise 1** ---

괄호 안의 단어를 활용하여 현재완료형 문장으로 영작하고 용법도 구별하세요.

1. 나는 그를 전에 만났던 적이 있다. (before)

→

2. 우리는 아직 저녁식사를 하지 않았다. (yet)

→

3. 나는 3년 전부터 이 회사에서 일해 왔다. (since)

→

4. 그 기차는 방금 떠났다. (just)

→

5. 그녀는 이미 그 영화를 봤다. (already)

→

6. 나는 그런 종류의 자동차를 전에 본 적이 없다. (before, that sort of)

→

---- **Exercise 1-1** --

다음을 괄호 안의 단어를 활용하여 현재완료형으로 영작하세요.

1. 나는 중국에 두 번 가봤다. (twice)

→

2. 나는 아직 나의 숙제를 끝내지 못했다. (yet)

→

3. 나는 그 배우를 만나본 적이 없다. (never)

→

4. 그 비행기는 막 도착했다. (just)

→

5. 나는 그곳에 이미 가봤다. (already, be there)

→

6. Jack은 그 곳에 한번 가봤다. (once)

→

unit 11 과거와 현재완료

: 과거는 과거에 종료된 일을, 현재완료는 과거에 시작된 일이 현재까지 영향을 미치는 일을 나타낸다.

- I lived in Seoul. (과거)

  나는 서울에 살았다. (지금은 살고 있는지 모름)

- I have lived in Seoul since I was 6. (현재완료)

  나는 내가 6살 때부터 지금까지 서울에 살아오고 있다. (지금도 살고 있음)

- I hated him. (과거)

  나는 그를 싫어했다. (지금도 싫어하는지 모름)

- I have hated him since that accident. (현재완료)

  나는 그 사건이후로 그를 싫어해오고 있다. (지금도 싫어함)

---- **Exercise 1** --

다음 괄호 안에 적절한 단어에 O표 하세요.

1. I went abroad with my brother (yesterday. / since yesterday.)

2. She admitted her mistake (three years ago. / for three years.)

3. Eric (saw / has seen) a super model in the street last year.

4. She (works / has worked) for this company for 5 years so far.

5. I have been to New York (yesterday./ before.)

---- **Exercise 1-1** --

다음 괄호 안에 적절한 단어에 O표 하세요.

1. The stone (was / has been) valuable so far.

2. I (went / have gone) to church last Sunday.

3. They (provided / have provided) food for homeless people last Sunday.

4. I (finished / have finished) my homework yesterday.

5. We have kept in touch with each other (for 10 years. / 10 years ago.)

Chapter 2 시제

1 다음 중 어법상 <u>틀린</u> 문장을 고르세요.

① Did you get my message?
② Did she finds her notebook?
③ Do they look delicious?
④ Were you late for school this morning?
⑤ Was the pen under the table?

2 다음 중 문법에 맞지 <u>않는</u> 문장은?

① I am having an English book.
② I was eating out then.
③ I went fishing yesterday.
④ I am singing a song now.
⑤ I went camping last week.

3 다음 중 어법상 옳은 문장은?

① I'm knowing Mary for 10 years.
② She is possessing an expensive necklace.
③ I'm believing you wouldn't do that.
④ The tourists are seeing the sights of New York.
⑤ This mansion is belonging to her.

[4-5] 다음 우리말과 일치하도록 빈칸에 알맞은 말을 쓰세요.

4

• 조심해! 차 한 대가 너를 향해 돌진하고 있어!
→ Watch out! A car_____
   toward you! (rush)

5

• 내가 잠에서 깼을 때 비가 오고 있었다.
→ It_____when I woke up.(rain)

6 다음 동사와 변화형이 잘못 짝지어진 것을 고르세요.

① go - went - gone
② lay(낳다) - laid - laid
③ find - founded - founded
④ take - took - taken
⑤ become - became - become

7 다음 중 동사의 변화가 바르지 <u>않은</u> 것은?

① read - read- read
② write -wrote - written
③ spend - spent - spent
④ drive - drove - droved
⑤ drink -drank- drunk

8 다음 문장과 의미가 같은 것은?

> Tom went to the USA, and he is not here.

① Tom has ever seen the USA.
② Tom has been to the USA.
③ Tom is used to going to the USA.
④ Tom has gone to the USA.
⑤ Tom used to go to the USA.

9 다음 빈칸에 들어갈 말로 알맞은 것은?

> Have you ever_____Mexican food?

① eat
② ate
③ to eat
④ eaten
⑤ eating

10 다음 주어진 문장을 괄호 안의 지시대로 고쳐 쓰세요.

(1)

> • Tom has fixed his car. (부정문으로)
>
> → _____.

(2)

> • Jack has watched TV. (의문문으로)
>
> → _____

11 다음 빈칸에 들어갈 말로 바르게 짝지어진 것은?

> A: Have you_____Minha since she came back from Tokyo?
>
> B: Yes, I_____her this evening.

① saw - saw
② saw - see
③ seen - seen
④ seen - seeing
⑤ seen - saw

[12-13] 우리말과 같은 뜻이 되도록 주어진 단어를 이용하여 문장을 완성하세요.

12 그 당시에 그는 과학 시험공부를 하고 있었다. (study for)

→ He_____his science test at that time.

13 엄마가 방문을 노크했을 때 나는 침대에서 쉬고 있었다. (take a rest)

→ I_____
on the bed when mom knocked on the door.

14 주어진 단어를 이용하여 대화를 완성하세요.

> A: How long_____(have, you) back pain?
> B: Since last Monday.
> A: What were you doing when you_____
> (hurt) your back?
> B: I_____(carry) a box on my shoulder.

15 다음 어법상 올바른 것은?

① I am born in 1998.
② She has received a birthday gift last week.
③ He lost his bag next month.
④ He founded the company in 2004.
⑤ I have met my best friend yesterday.

16 다음 빈칸에 들어갈 말로 바르게 짝지어진 것을 고르세요.

> How long_____you_____English?

① were-studied
② was- studying
③ did-studied
④ have-studied
⑤ have-studying

17 다음 중 밑줄 친 부분과 쓰임이 같은 것은?

> I have lived here for a year.

① I have once met her.
② He has just arrived here.
③ Somebody has taken my bag.
④ Tom has finished his homework.
⑤ We have been good friends since we were young.

18 다음 빈칸에 들어갈 말로 알맞지 않은 것은?

> I got an A+ on math test_____.

① last week
② yesterday
③ a few weeks later
④ today
⑤ a year ago

19 다음 문장에서 밑줄 친 부분을 문법에 맞게 고치세요.

> He didn't do his homework since then.
>
> → _____.

20 다음 문장의 빈칸에 들어갈 말로 알맞은 것은?

My daughter_____English literature.

① is hating
② is liking
③ is knowing
④ is seeing
⑤ is studying

21 다음 우리말과 일치 하도록 빈칸에 알맞은 말을 쓰세요.

(1) Kate는 시장에 가고 없다.

→ Kate_____to the market.

(2) Kate는 시장에 가본 적이 있다.

→ Kate_____to the market.

22 다음 문장의 빈칸을 주어진 단어의 형태를 적절히 바꿔 채우세요.

I_____to letting children stay late since the accident. (object)

23 다음 밑줄 친 부분의 용법이 나머지 넷과 다른 것은?

① I've never been to Rome.
② Have you ever been to Japan?
③ She has just been to the station.
④ I have been to Mt. Halla once.
⑤ He has been to America twice.

24 다음 중 현재완료의 용법이 보기와 같은 것을 고르세요.

Have you ever seen a spaceship?

① It has rained since yesterday.
② I have never heard of her name.
③ Mr. Kim has gone to the U.S.
④ He has already drawn a pretty picture.
⑤ She hasn't read the funny book yet.

25 다음 중 어법상 틀린 문장을 고르세요.

① I'm leaving tonight.
② My sister has lost her purse.
③ You lived here since last year.
④ I have not met my friend yet.
⑤ I received your letter this morning.

3 조동사
Chapter

Gorilla Grammar

unit 12 can, may, will

: 조동사는 동사 앞에 놓여 동사가 나타내는 뜻을 보조하는 역할을 하며 단독 사용은 하지 않는다.
조동사는 능력, 의무, 추측, 가능, 습관 등의 뜻을 포함하여 어감을 풍부하게 해준다.

- -

★ **조동사 기본 사항**

a. 조동사 뒤에는 동사원형이 온다.

- She can plays the guitar. (X)
- She can play the guitar. (O)

  그녀는 기타를 칠 수 있다.

b. 접속사를 쓰지 않는 경우 한 문장에는 조동사 한 개만 사용한다.

- She will can do that. (x)
- She will be able to do that. (o)

  그녀는 그것을 할 수 있을 것이다.

c. 부정문과 의문문을 만들 때 조동사를 활용한다.

- She can doesn't play the piano. (X)
- She can't (cannot) play the piano. (O)

  그녀는 피아노를 연주할 수 없다.

- Can she play the piano? (O)

  그녀는 피아노를 연주할 수 있을까?

허락과 허가의 조동사 can, may

: 허락을 맡거나 허가를 내려줄 때 사용. may는 의문문에서 1인칭일 때만 사용. 그 때 may와 can은 서로
교체가능하다. 이 때 과거형(could, might)는 과거를 나타내는 것이 아니고 좀 더 공손한 표현이 된다.

- You can(may) go to the concert.

  너는 콘서트에 가도 된다.

- You can(may) play computer games until midnight.

  너는 자정까지 컴퓨터 게임을 해도 된다.

unit 12 can, may, will

- Can you help me?
- May you help me? (x)

  너는 나를 도울 수 있니?

- Can(May) I eat the hamburger?

  햄버거를 먹어도 될까요?

- -Yes, you can(may). /No, you can't(may not).

  응, 그래. /아니, 안 돼.

2 능력의 조동사 can

: '~할 수 있다'라고 해석된다. 과거의 능력을 나타낼 때는 could를 쓰면 된다.
또한, 'be able to동사원형'으로 바꿔 쓸 수 있다.

- I can handle this problem.
= I am able to handle this problem.

  나는 이 문제를 해결할 수 있다.

- She can speak French.

  그녀는 프랑스어로 말할 수 있다.

3 추측의 조동사 may

: 가능성을 담은 추측을 할 때 사용하며, '~일지도 모른다', 정도로 해석한다.

- He may get up late.

  그는 늦게 일어날지도 모른다.

unit 12 can, may, will

4 미래의 조동사 will

a. 미래의 일에 대해 말하거나 예측할 때, '~일 것이다'로 해석된다.

- He will have a girlfriend someday.

  그는 언젠가 여자친구를 사귈 것이다.

- 좀 더 예정된 미래는 'be going to V'

5 의지의 조동사 will

a. 주어의 의지를 나타낼 때, '~할 것이다', '~하려고 한다.'로 해석된다.

- She will pass the exam.

  그녀는 그 시험에 통과할 것이다.

- They will leave him.

  그들은 그를 떠나려고 한다.

b. Will you~? 제안 또는 요청할 때 사용. '~해주실래요?'라고 해석된다.

- Will you join us?

  우리와 함께 할래요?

- Will you marry me?

  저와 결혼해주실래요?

---- **Exercise 1** --

다음 문장을 해석하세요.

1. My heart will go on.

2. How will the weather be like on Wednesday?

3. Could you do me a favor?

4. Would you mind gathering together?

5. Could you please take a picture for us?

6. What can you do for me?

7. Some people will offer you some cookies.

8. May I call you later?

9. Can you speak French?

다음 문장을 해석하세요.

1. One day, she will come back.

2. The private airplane will satisfy you.

3. We can reduce greenhouse gases by recycling waste.

4. He can't solve the problem alone.

5. Can I leave a message?

6. We will play with the toys.

7. My life will be easy and happy as time goes on.

---- **Exercise 2** ---

다음 조동사 can, may, will의 용법으로 알맞은 것에 O표 하세요.

1. May I leave now? (허가 / 추측)

2. Can you speak German? (능력·가능 / 허가)

3. I will do my best. (단순미래 / 의지미래)

4. This book may be helpful to you. (허가 / 추측)

5. They can solve the problems without a teacher. (능력·가능 / 허가)

6. She may know the truth. Let me ask her. (허가 / 추측)

7. You can go out with him if you finish your homework. (능력·가능 / 허가)

8. Can I help you? (능력·가능 / 허가)

9. I cannot clean my room right now. (능력·가능 / 허가)

---- **Exercise 2-1** --

다음 조동사 can, may, will의 용법으로 알맞은 것에 O표 하세요.

1. May I write a letter with this pen? (허가 / 추측)

2. She can unlock the door by herself. (능력 · 가능 /허가)

3. It will be dark soon. (단순미래 / 의지미래)

4. You can go now. (능력 · 가능 / 허가)

5. May I use your laptop? (허가 / 추측)

6. Can you swim faster than a fish? (능력 · 가능 / 허가)

7. I will solve this problem by myself. (단순미래 / 의지미래)

8. This news may not be true. (허가 / 추측)

EXERCISE

같은 의미의 문장이 되도록 (   ) 안에 적절한 단어를 쓰세요.

1. She can come here.
   = She (   ) (   ) (   ) come here.

2. Can you finish this work by tomorrow?
   = (   ) you (   ) (   ) finish this work by tomorrow?

3. He is not able to speak slowly.
   = He (   ) (   )speak slowly.

4. Kate is able to run very fast.
   = Kate (   ) run very fast.

5. I will go to the movies with Jane tomorrow.
   = I (   ) (   ) (   ) go to the movies with Jane tomorrow.

---- **Exercise 3-1** --

같은 의미의 문장이 되도록 (   ) 안에 적절한 단어를 쓰세요.

1. John can play the piano very well.

= John (   ) (   ) (   ) play the piano very well.

2. They can't speak Korean fluently.

= They (   ) (   ) (   ) (   ) speak Korean fluently.

3. Tom will take an important exam soon.

= Tom (   ) (   ) (   ) take an important exam soon.

4. 1 am going to go to the hospital tomorrow.

= 1 (   ) go to the hospital tomorrow.

5. 1 cannot remember her address.

= 1 (   ) (   ) (   ) (   ) remember her address.

EXERCISE

다음 주어진 문장을 영작하세요.

1. 너는 영어로 말할 수 있니?

    →

2. 제가 도와드릴까요?

    →

3. 나는 최선을 다 할 것이다. (do one's best)

    →

4. 편지를 이 연필로 적어도 되나요?

    →

5. 이 영화는 그들에게 매우 재미있을지도 모른다. (fun)

    →

6. 그녀는 빨리 달릴 수 있다. (fast)

    →

7. 내일 여기로 올 수 있나요?

    →

8. 너희들은 내 강의를 충분히 이해할 수 있니? (lecture)

    →

9. 그는 언젠가 스마트폰을 살 것이다. (someday)

    →

---- **Exercise 4-1** --

다음 주어진 문장을 영작하세요.

1. 나는 스페인어를 할 줄 모른다.

→

2. 이 영화는 너에게 지루할지도 모른다. (boring)

→

3. 내일 여기로 올 거니?

→

4. 내가 네 사전을 사용해도 되겠니? (dictionary)

→

5. 너 혼자 이 지역을 보호할 수 있니? (area)

→

6. Kate는 내년에 30살이 될 것이다. (be thirty)

→

7. 너는 이제 집에 가도 좋다.

→

8. 나는 다시는 그것을 하지 않을 것이다.

→

9. 그는 그의 감정을 통제하게 될 것이다. (emotion, control)

→

unit 13 must, have to, should

 must

a. 의무를 나타내는 must

: 중요성, 구속력 있는 의무를 나타낼 때 사용 '~해야만 한다'로 해석

• You **must keep** the rules.

너는 규칙을 지켜야한다.

b. 강한 추측을 나타내는 must

: 큰 확신을 가지고 추측할 때 사용 '~임에 틀림없다'로 해석

• She **must be** angry.

그녀는 화가났음에 틀림없다.

★★ 강한 추측의 부정은 must not 이 아닌 can't (cannot)으로 사용.

• She **can't be** angry.

그녀가 화났을 리가 없다.

 have to

a. 의무를 나타내는 have to: '해야만 한다'로 해석되며 must와 바꿔 쓸 수 있다.

• You **must keep** the rules.

≒ You **have to keep** the rules.

너는 규칙을 지켜야만 한다.

• She **must pass** the exam.

≒ She **has to pass** the exam.

그녀는 시험에 통과해야 한다.

☆ must가 좀 더 구속력을 가진다.

unit 13 must, have to, should

3 should (= ought to)

a. 의무를 나타내는 should

: '~해야만 한다'로 해석되지만 must나 have to보다 강제성이 덜하며 권고에 가까운
표현을 원할 때 사용한다.

• You **should** keep the rules.

너는 규칙을 지켜야한다.

4 must와 should, have to의 부정문

a. must not: ~해서는 안 된다.

• You **must not** follow the guy.(그 남자는 위험한 사람이야.)

너는 그 남자를 따라서는 안 된다.

b. should not: ~해서는 안된다. (= ought not to+v)

• You **should not** follow the guy. (그 남자는 괴짜야.)

너는 그 남자를 따라서는 안된다.

c. don't have to: ~할 필요가 없다. (= don't need to)

• You **don't have to** follow the guy because I can help you.

너는 그 남자를 따를 필요가 없다. 내가 도와줄 수 있기 때문에.

EXERCISE

---- **Exercise 1** ---

다음 문장의 의미가 비슷하도록 빈칸을 채우세요.

1. I must do it right now.
= I (   ) (   ) do it right now.

2. She should obey the rule.
= She (   ) (   ) obey the rule.

3. She has to follow my instructions.
= She (   ) follow my instructions.

4. The show must go on.
= The show (   ) (   ) go on.

5. Children should listen to their parents.
= Children (   ) (   ) listen to their parents.

90 | Junior Gorilla Grammar   Level 2

---- **Exercise 1-1** --

다음 문장의 의미가 비슷하도록 빈칸을 채우세요.

1. People must stay inside.
= People (   ) (   ) stay inside.

2. You should thank God for still being alive.
= You (   ) (   ) thank God for still being alive.

3. He must finish the report until tomorrow morning.
= He (   ) (   ) finish the report until tomorrow morning.

4. The teacher should advise Tom not to be late.
= The teacher (   ) (   ) advise Tom not to be late.

5. I ought to take care of her.
= I (   ) take care of her.

EXERCISE

다음 문장에서 must의 용법으로 적절한 것에 O표 하세요.

1. She must be a foreigner. (필요, 의무 / 강한추측)

2. You must not go there without permission. (필요, 의무 / 강한추측)

3. He must respect his teacher. (필요, 의무 / 강한추측)

4. She must be very upset because of me. (필요, 의무 / 강한추측)

5. You must be kidding! (필요, 의무 / 강한추측)

6. You must feel homesick around this time of the year. (필요, 의무 /강한추측)

7. We must do our best. (필요, 의무 / 강한추측)

8. She must do her work at once. (필요, 의무 / 강한추측)

9. Tom must be popular in school because he is so handsome. (필요, 의무 / 강한추측)

10. Man must live by the sweat of his brow. (필요, 의무 / 강한추측)

---- **Exercise 3** ---

다음 문장을 단순히 부정문으로 바꾸고 그에 맞게 해석하세요.

1. You have to work at the factory.

→

2. We should grab the chances.

→

3. She must clean her room.

→

4. We must follow his direction.

→

5. I should feed my cat.

→

---- **Exercise 3-1** ---

다음 문장을 단순히 부정문으로 바꾸고 그에 맞게 해석하세요.

1. You must increase the sales of the company.

→

2. You have to tell me everything about Jane.

→

3. We should listen to them carefully.

→

4. We ought to speak in English here.

→

5. They must finish this project as soon as possible.

→

unit 14 used to, would

: used to와 would는 모두 과거의 습관을 나타낸다.

used to : 과거의 규칙적인 습관이나 상태를 나타낸다.

- There used to be a big tree.
  거기에 큰 나무가 있곤 했다.
- I used to have a boyfriend.
  나는 남자 친구가 있곤 했다.

would: 과거의 불규칙한 습관을 나타낸다.

- I would sing a song
  나는 노래를 부르곤했다. (불규칙적으로)

- We would often go fishing together.
  우리는 종종 낚시에 함께 가곤 했다. (불규칙적으로)
- We used to go fishing together every Saturday.
  우리는 매주 토요일마다 함께 낚시에 가곤 했다. (규칙적으로)

---- **Exercise 1** --

다음 주어진 문장을 영작하세요.

1. 나는 일본에 살곤 했다.
→

2. 나는 일요일마다 집에 머무르곤 했다.
→

3. 나는 친구들과 종종 축구하고 놀곤 했다. (sometimes)
→

4. 그는 자주 아침에 늦잠을 자곤 했다. (often)
→

5. 거기에 높은 빌딩 하나가 있곤 했다. (tall building, over)
→

---- **Exercise 1-1** --

다음 주어진 문장을 영작하세요.

1. 나는 방에서 혼자 노래를 부르곤 했다.
→

2. 그는 그들에게 토요일마다 전화하곤 했다.
→

3. 그는 매일 저녁 샤워를 하곤 했다. (take a shower)
→

4. 나는 가족과 같이 살곤 했다.
→

Exercise 1

다음 주어진 문장을 영작하세요.

1. 너희들은 그녀에게 인사해야 한다. (should, say hello to)

→

2. 너는 그것을 지금 당장 해야 한다. (have to)

→

3. 그는 나보다 어린 게 틀림없다.

→

4. 너는 이 책을 읽을 필요는 없다.

→

5. 이 편지를 이 펜으로 적어도 되나요?

→

6. 제가 그 곳에 내일 가야만 하나요? (have to)

→

7. 너는 술을 너무 많이 마시면 안 된다. (should)

→

8. 너는 지금 당장 Jane에게 전화해야 한다. (have to)

→

Exercise 1-2

다음 주어진 문장을 영작하세요.

1. 그녀는 하루 종일 걸어야 한다. (has to)

→

2. 그는 그 방에 허가 없이 들어갈 수 있다. (permission)

→

3. 너는 그 빵을 그와 나눠 먹을 수 있니? (share)

→

4. 그는 그녀를 신뢰할 것이다. (trust)

→

5. 내가 네 사전을 사용해도 되겠니? (may)

→

6. 너는 그 규칙들을 지켜야만 한다.

→

7. 내가 이 책을 읽어야만 하나요?

→

8. 제가 그 상품을 광고해도 될까요? (can, advertise)

→

9. 나는 그 나무에 오를 수 있다.

→

Exercise 1-3

다음 주어진 문장을 영작하세요.

1. Kate는 내년에 고등학교를 졸업할 것이다. (graduate from)

→

2. 제가 연필로 편지를 써도 됩니까?(may)

→

3. 내일 여기로 올 수 있나요?(will)

→

4. 너는 어제 그 파티에 갔니?

→

5. 우리가 위기를 극복할 수 있을까? (the crisis, overcome)

→

6. 나는 다시는 그것을 하지 않을 것이다.

→

7. 너는 중간고사를 준비해야 한다. (should, the mid-term exam)

→

8. 너는 너무 많이 먹으면 안 된다. (should)

→

1 다음 문장의 빈칸에 들어갈 말로 알맞은 것을 고르세요.

> I'm going on a diet. I_____eat after eight o'clock in the evening.

① should
② must
③ don't have to
④ can
⑤ won't

2 다음 문장에서 **틀린** 부분을 찾아 고치세요.

> She can plays the piano.

3 다음 문장에서 어법상 **틀린** 것은?

> I think you should wrote down
> ①   ②   ③
> the things to buy.
> ④   ⑤

4 다음 우리말과 일치하도록 할 때 빈칸에 들어갈 말로 바르게 짝지어 진 것은?

> • 그녀는 화났을지도 몰라.
> → She_____be angry.
>
> • 그녀는 화난 것이 틀림없어.
> → She_____be angry.
>
> • 그녀는 화났을 리가 없어.
> → She_____be angry.

① may - must - may
② must - cannot -may
③ must - may - cannot
④ may - must - cannot
⑤ cannot - may - must

5 다음 중 밑줄 친 부분과 쓰임이 같은 것은?

> I may go to the grocery store to buy some milk.

① You may come in.
② May I come here?
③ May I use this pen?
④ You may take a rest.
⑤ It may rain this Sunday.

6 다음 내용과 의미가 같은 것은?

> There were many flowers in front of my house, but there aren't any flowers now.

① There used to be many flowers in front of my house.
② There must be many flowers in front of my house.
③ There have to be many flowers in front of my house.
④ There can be many flowers in front of my house.
⑤ There were able to be many flowers in front of my house.

7 다음 우리말과 일치하도록 빈칸에 알맞은 말을 쓰세요.

> • 그녀는 내게 "그것은 사실일 리가 없다."라고 말했다.
> → She said to me, " It_____ _____true."

8 다음 중 어법상 올바른 것은?

① I am able to play the violin.
② Can she speaks Japanese well?
③ You will can help your mother.
④ We are able to play soccer yesterday.
⑤ I don't able to find my book.

9 다음 중 빈칸에 have to가 들어가기에 가장 적절하지 <u>않은</u> 것은?

① We_____do our best.
② Do you_____go now?
③ They_____be very busy.
④ She will_____do it tomorrow.
⑤ Do I_____finish my homework now?

10 다음 문장을 미래시제의 문장으로 고쳐 쓸 때 빈칸에 알맞은 말을 쓰세요.

> • He must get up early.
>
> → He_____ _____ _____get up early next week.

11 다음 글의 빈칸에 들어갈 말로 알맞은 것은?

> Mark is going to go camping tomorrow. The bus leaves at 7 a.m. His mom told him "You_____go to bed early. You have to get up very early tomorrow."

① don't
② would
③ had better
④ could
⑤ must not

12 다음 중 밑줄 친 <u>must</u>의 쓰임이 나머지 넷과 가장 <u>다른</u> 것은?

① He <u>must</u> be tired.
② You <u>must</u> do it right now.
③ <u>Must</u> I dress up for the party?
④ She <u>must</u> get up early not to be late.
⑤ They <u>must</u> finish the game.

13 다음 문장의 빈칸에 공통으로 알맞은 조동사를 쓰세요.

• _____ I open the door?
• She_____ speak four different languages.

[14-15] 주어진 우리말을 영어로 옮길 때 빈칸에 알맞은 표현으로 채우세요.

14

• 10년 전에는 이곳에 작은 가게들이 많이 있었다.

→ There_____ be a lot of small stores here 10 years ago.

15

• 그녀는 착한 척을 할 필요가 없다.

→ She_____ pretend to be kind.

16 다음 대화의 빈칸에 들어갈 말로 알맞은 것을 고르세요.

A: I'll wait in line for tickets.
B: We _____ stand in line.
   I already booked our tickets.

① don't have to
② should not
③ would rather
④ ought to
⑤ need to

17 다음 빈칸에 적절한 조동사를 써넣으세요.

He_____ lift the box. I have seen him lift the box before.

18 다음 문장이 우리말에 맞도록 빈칸에 알맞은 말을 쓰세요.

• 지금 집에 가도 되나요?

Can l go home now?
= _____ l go home now?

19 다음 중 어법상 맞는 문장은?

① She may be not Korean.
② My computer might have a problem.
③ She can eats some food if she is hungry.
④ My father may came late yesterday.
⑤ He can talking to strangers.

20 다음 대화의 빈칸에 들어갈 말이 순서대로 짝 지어진 것은?

A: _____you play the piano?
B: l _____play it when l was an elementary school student, but now l can't.

① Can - could
② May- might
③ May - may not
④ Can - can't
⑤ May - could

4 수동태
Chapter

- unit 15. 수동태

- unit 16. 수동태의 여러 형태

Gorilla Grammar

unit 15 수동태

1 능동태와 수동태

a. 능동태: 주인공이 직접 행동을 하는 것을 말한다.

- They love him.

  그들은 그를 사랑한다.

- I cleaned the room.

  나는 그 방을 치웠다.

b. 수동태: 목적어가 주어가 되어 행위를 당하거나 영향을 받을 때 사용

기본형태	주어 + be동사 + p.p. + (by 행위자)

★ 밑줄 친 be 동사에서 시제 변환

- He <u>is</u> loved by them.

  그는 그들에 의해서 사랑받는다.

- The room <u>was</u> cleaned by me.

  그 방은 나에 의해서 치워졌다.

부정문	주어 + be동사 + not + p.p. + (by 행위자)

★ 부정문을 만들 때 be동사 뒤에 not을 붙인다.

- He is not loved by them.

  그는 그들에 의해서 사랑받지 않는다.

의문문	be동사 + 주어 + p.p ~ ?

- Is he loved by them?

  그는 그들에 의해서 사랑받니?

unit 15 수동태

2 「by 행위자」의 생략

: 행위자가 일반인이거나 중요하지 않을 경우, 그리고 분명하지 않은 경우에는 「by 행위자」를 생략한다.

- Japanese is spoken in Japan.

  일본어는 일본에서 말하여진다.

- The coffee cup was broken.

  그 커피 잔은 깨졌다.

- The lilies were painted pink.

  그 백합들은 핑크색으로 칠해졌다.

3 수동태의 시제

a. 현재: <u>am /are /is + p.p. + (by 행위자)</u>

- The cat is led by a little mouse.

  그 고양이는 작은 쥐에 의해서 이끌어진다.

- A bike is fixed by a repairman.

  자전거는 수리공에 의해서 고쳐진다.

b. 과거: <u>was /were + p.p. + (by 행위자)</u>

- The cat was led by a little mouse.

  그 고양이는 작은 쥐에 의해 이끌어졌다.

- The bike was fixed by the repairman.

  그 자전거는 그 수리공에 의해서 고쳐졌다.

c. 조동사: <u>조동사 + be + p.p. + (by 행위자)</u>

- The cat cannot be led by a little mouse.

  그 고양이는 작은 쥐에 의해서 이끌어질 수 없다.

- The bike will be fixed by the repairman.

  그 자전거는 그 수리공에 의해서 고쳐질 것이다.

EXERCISE

다음 주어진 능동태 문장을 수동태로 바꾸세요.

1. They love him.

→

2. The little mouse leads the tiger.

→

3. Americans speak English.

→

4. My grandmother grows a tree.

→

5. The birds play the piano.

→

6. He cleans the garden every day.

→

7. They break windows.

→

8. He uses the machine effectively.

→

9. A sponge absorbs water.

→

10. Poly delays her every task.

→

---- **Exercise 1-1** --

다음 주어진 능동태 문장을 수동태로 바꾸세요.

1. Kim wrote the novel in 1993.

→

2. She will eat a hamburger.

→

3. They broke the barrier.

→

4. Her sister can fix the bike.

→

5. They sold the roses at a low price.

→

6. She served the coffee.

→

7. He built this building in 2001.

→

8. King Sejong invented Hanguel.

→

9. She will cut the paper.

→

10. Kelly painted the wall.

→

---- **Exercise 1-2** --

다음 주어진 능동태 문장을 수동태로 바꾸세요.

1. The army attacked the town at dawn.

→

2. They will buy lots of books.

→

3. She raises a cute cat.

→

4. John built a building.

→

5. We can buy the expensive car.

→

6. Brad should finish the report within this week.

→

7. I changed my decision yesterday.

→

8. We will fix the door today.

→

9. They sell cookies on the street.

→

10. Susan will break the machine.

→

---- **Exercise 2** --

다음 문장을 수동태는 능동태로, 능동태는 수동태로 변환하세요.

1. Tom writes a book.

→

2. The problem can be solved by her.

→

3. He ate all the apples.

→

4. Jane is taught by Tom.

→

5. Mr. Yang will direct this movie.

→

6. Sophie played the violin.

→

7. My room is not cleaned by my mom.

→

8. I clean the yard every day.

→

9. Minsu founded a school.

→

10. John broke her cup.

→

EXERCISE

다음 문장을 수동태는 능동태로, 능동태는 수동태로 변환하세요.

1. Somebody stole my watch.

→

2. They clean the floor every Monday.

→

3. The vase was broken by Tom.

→

4. The class is canceled by the teacher.

→

5. The Internet is used by many people nowadays.

→

6. You should obey this rule.

→

7. Da Vinci painted the Mona Lisa.

→

8. We can see stars in the sky.

→

9. He didn't invite Sally to the party.

→

10. The cars are sold at a high price by them.

→

---- **Exercise 3** ---

다음 괄호 안에 옳은 형태에 O표 하세요.

1. This picture was painted by (he / hers / me).

2. By (where / whom / whose) was the English made?

3. He (doesn't / isn't / won't) invited to the party.

4. Are these cars (making / made / makes) in Germany?

5. When (was / did / does) this building built?

---- **Exercise 3-1** ---

다음 괄호 안에 옳은 형태에 O표 하세요.

1. A : Is English spoken in Australia?
   B : (Yes, it does. / Yes, it is.)

2. These books are (writing / written / wrote) in Japanese.

3. She is (locking / locked / locks) up in the bathroom.

4. She actually (known / know / knew) everyone.

5. The wall of the house was (paints / painted / painting) by Lauren.

---- **Exercise 4** ---

다음 주어진 단어를 활용해서 문장을 영작하세요.

1. 나는 너에게 맞았다. (hit)

→

2. 그는 선생님에 의해 별실에 배치되었다. (place in / separate room)

→

3. 그 방식은 그에 의해 발견되었다. (find)

→

4. 전화기는 Alexander Bell에 의해 발명되었다. (invent)

→

5. 다리는 강 위에 건설되었다. (build)

→

6. 이 소설은 Tom에 의해 쓰였다. (write)

→

---- **Exercise 4-1** --

다음 주어진 단어를 활용해서 문장을 영작하세요.

1. 이 노래들은 JYS에 의해 불려진다. (sing)

→

2. 이 테이블은 누구에 의해 만들어졌어? (make)

→

3. 그 가수는 모두에게 알려져 있다. (know to)

→

4. 너는 분노에 의해 파괴될 것이다. (destroy, rage)

→

5. 이 운동화는 일본에서 만들어진다. (make)

→

6. 이 교실은 매일 그녀에 의해 청소된다. (clean)

→

unit 16 수동태의 여러 형태

 4형식과 5형식의 수동태

a. 4형식의 수동태

: 4형식은 목적어를 2개 가지기 때문에 2종류의 수동태가 가능하다.

하지만, 어색한 경우는 사용하지 않는다.

★ 직접목적어가 주어가 되는 경우 전치사가 필요하다.

- I teach her English
→ She is taught English by me.
→ English is taught to her by me.

- She cooked me pizza last night.
→ ~~I was cooked pizza last night by her.~~ (어색함)
→ Pizza was cooked for me last night by her.

- -
★ 전치사 선택 방법: 4형식 문장을 3형식으로 바꿀 때 쓰는 전치사를 써준다.

전치사 to를 필요로 하는 동사	give, teach, tell, show 등
전치사 for를 필요로 하는 동사	buy, make, get 등
전치사 of를 필요로 하는 동사	ask 등

b. 5형식의 수동태: 5형식은 목적어가 주어자리에 가면 목적보어가 남아서 주격보어가 된다.
- I made him happy.
→ He was made <u>happy</u> (by me).

---- **Exercise 1** --

다음 문장을 수동태로 바꾸세요. (정답이 한 개일 수도 있음)

1. Minji showed us a beautiful vase.

→

→

2. She bought him a watch.

→

→

3. They sent me a present.

→

→

4. We made him sad.

→

→

5. I asked him a question.

→

→

EXERCISE

다음 문장을 수동태로 바꾸세요. (정답이 한 개일 수도 있음)

1. Kim calls me Jane.
→

→

2. He sometimes makes me spaghetti.
→

→

3. He teaches children Japanese.
→

→

4. Suzy got him a smartphone.
→

→

5. You got her upset.
→

→

unit 16 수동태의 여러 형태

2 by 이외의 전치사를 사용하는 수동태

be interested in	~에 흥미가 있다
be involved in	~에 관련되다, 연루되다
be covered with (in)	~로 덮여있다
be filled with (of)	~로 가득 차다
be pleased with	~로 기뻐하다
be satisfied with	~에 만족하다
be disappointed with (at)	~에 실망하다
be surprised at	~에 놀라다
be worried about	~을 걱정하다
be tired of	~에 싫증나다
be tired from	~ 때문에 지치다
be known to	~에게 알려지다
be known as	~로서 유명하다
be known for	~로 유명하다
be made of	~로 만들어지다 (물리적 변화)
be made from	~로 만들어지다 (화학적 변화)
be made in	~에서 만들어지다

EXERCISE

다음 괄호 안에 적절한 단어에 O표 하세요.

1. I am worried (about / for / to) your health.

2. The box is filled (for / to / with) paper.

3. We were so pleased (to / in / with) the gifts.

4. The whole hill is covered (of / to / with) cherry blossoms.

5. He is tired (from / of / for) eating the same food every day.

6. They are known (as / to / for) people in Thailand.

7. I'm interested (in / at / for) math.

8. These clothes were made (in / of / from) the finest silk.

9. She is surprised (in / at / for) Tom's rudeness.

10. This shirt is made (of / on / in) Korea.

---- **Exercise 2** --

다음 빈칸을 주어진 단어를 활용하여 채우세요.

1. I_____ his mother. (worry, 현재)

2. He_____a pop singer. (know, 현재)

3. The doctor_____everybody. (know, 현재)

4. I_____ watching the boring play. (tire, 현재)

5. My dad_____my score. (satisfy, 현재)

6. _____you_____swimming? (interest, 현재)

7. The mayor_____the scandal. (involve, 과거)

8. The road _____ cars. (fill, 과거)

9. You should_____ yourself to do so. (please)

10. Gang-nam_____too many cars yesterday. (crowd, 과거)

Chapter 4 수동태

1 다음 문장의 빈칸에 들어갈 말로 알맞은 것은?

My younger sister_____to the hospital
for treatment yesterday.

① is sent
② send
③ was sent
④ sent
⑤ was sending

[2-3] 다음 대화의 빈칸에 들어갈 말로 알맞은 것을 고르세요.

2

A: Who wrote Harry Potter?
B: It_____by J.K.Rowling.

① is written
② was written
③ is writing
④ was writing
⑤ has written

3

A: Oh! I forgot to turn the key in the lock.
B: Don't worry. It_____off.

① is turning
② already turned
③ already turns
④ was already turned
⑤ were already turned

4 다음 괄호 안의 단어를 알맞은 형태로 바꿔 현재시제로 빈칸에 쓰세요.

(1) My brother_____the dog every morning.
(feed)

(2) The dog_____by my older brother
every morning. (feed)

[5-6] 다음 문장의 빈칸에 들어갈 알맞은 전치사를 쓰세요.

5 She was not pleased_____her work.

6 Cake is made_____flour, milk and eggs.

[7-8] 다음 우리말을 영어로 바르게 옮긴 것을 고르세요.

7

개는 레스토랑에서 허용되어서는 안 된다.

① Dogs are not permitted in a restaurant.
② Dogs should be not permitted in a restaurant.
③ Dogs should not be permitted in a restaurant.
④ Dogs are permitted not in a restaurant.
⑤ Dogs are not permitted by a restaurant.

8

숙제는 이번 주 금요일까지 완성되어야 한다.

① The homework must be finish by this Friday.
② The homework must finish by this Friday.
③ The homework must be finished by this Friday.
④ The homework must have finished by this Friday.
⑤ The homework must be finishing by this Friday.

[9-10] 다음 문장에서 어법상 틀린 부분을 찾아 바르게 고쳐 쓰세요.

9 The necklace was stole yesterday.

10 Is the necklace love by you?

[11-12] 다음 중 어법상 틀린 문장을 고르세요.

11
① The car door was opened by her.
② This news article was written by my younger sister.
③ My father wrote me a long letter.
④ This road built with trees by my older sister.
⑤ The window was broken by the children.

12
① I was taken to the park by my friend.
② The company was founded by her in 1991.
③ The newspaper was written by them.
④ The cereals made by Mr.tiger.
⑤ The dish was prepared by my mom.

[13-15] 다음 괄호 안에서 알맞은 것을 고르세요.

13 A top chef (runs / is run) the restaurant.

14 The flowerpot (brought / was brought) by my mother.

15 My friend (passed / was passed) by my house.

[16-17] 다음 두 문장이 같은 뜻이 되도록 빈칸에 알맞은 말을 쓰세요.

16 Many people use subway stations every day.

→ Subway stations_____by many people every day.

17 People call me Emily.

→ I_____Emily by people.

18 다음 중 주어진 문장과 가장 의미가 통하는 문장을 고르세요.

| The food was eaten by the dog. |

① The food was not eaten by the dog.
② The food ate the dog.
③ The food and the dog were eaten.
④ The dog ate the food.
⑤ What the dog ate is another food.

19 다음 중 어법상 맞는 문장을 고르세요.

① My parents took us to the theater.
② The ring is keeping by my mother.
③ The cake was baked my mother.
④ The love song was sing by my younger sister.
⑤ She is played the game.

20 다음 중 어법상 맞는 문장을 고르세요.

① I was surprised my math grade.
② Dad was watched a football game.
③ The toy made by the company.
④ His body was placed inside a pyramid.
⑤ The treasure discovered by the explorer.

21 다음 문장을 수동태 문장으로 바르게 고친 것은?

| What do you call this in Arabic? |

① What do this called in Arabic?
② What this is called in Arabic?
③ What is this called in Arabic?
④ Does this called what in Arabic?
⑤ Does what called this in Arabic?

22 다음 밑줄 친 부분을 수동의 형태로 바르게 고쳐 쓴 것은?

| This glass can <u>break</u> easily. |

① broke
② breaking
③ broken
④ be broken
⑤ be break

23 다음 중 어법상 <u>틀린</u> 문장을 모두 고른 것은?

ⓐ The public morals must be kept by the public.
ⓑ Did the question be understood by everyone?
ⓒ Black pepper was discovered not by american.
ⓓ Her homework may not finished by her.

① ⓐ, ⓓ
② ⓑ, ⓓ
③ ⓒ, ⓓ
④ ⓐ, ⓑ, ⓒ
⑤ ⓑ, ⓒ, ⓓ

24 다음 중 문장의 전환이 <u>잘못된</u> 것은?

① Did anyone see Minsoo?
→ Was Minsoo seen by anyone?
② We must do something for this homework.
→ Something must be done by us for this homework.
③ He didn't draw the landscape.
→ The landscape was not drawn by him.
④ The novel may move him.
→ He may be moved by the novel.
⑤ Where did you find this artifact?
→ Was this artifact found by you where?

25 다음 문장을 수동태로 바꿔 쓰세요.

(1) We can see lots of stars at night.

→ _____

(2) My sister drank water after jogging.

→ _____

5 to부정사
Chapter

Gorilla Grammar

unit 17 to부정사의 명사적 용법

: 원래는 동사였지만 다른 역할을 하고 싶을 때 동사 앞에 to를 붙여서 명사, 형용사, 부사의 역할을 할 수 있으며 이러한 형태를 to부정사라 한다.

★ to부정사가 명사역할을 할 때, 명사처럼 주어, 목적어, 보어자리에 들어갈 수 있다.

1 주어 역할

- **To relax after an exam is necessary.**
  시험 후에 쉬는 것은 필수적이다.

- **To have a surprise party is our plan.**
  깜짝 파티를 여는 것이 우리의 계획이다.

2 보어 역할

- **His plan is to get closer to the man.**
  그의 계획은 그 남자에게 접근하는 것이다.

- **Her aim is to take a picture of the famous actor.**
  그녀의 목표는 그 유명한 배우의 사진을 찍는 것이다.

3 목적어 역할

- **He wanted to hold her bag.**
  그는 그녀의 가방을 들어주길 원했다.

- **She decided to give a chance.**
  그녀는 기회를 한 번 주기로 결심했다.

EXERCISE

다음 주어진 문장을 문법에 맞게 고치세요.

1. Study math is not easy.

2. My hobby is collect stamps.

3. She likes cook.

4. Be a doctor is difficult.

5. The mission was take pictures of her.

6. I want make up with him.

7. Stay healthy is important.

8. Tell a lie is the worst thing in a relationship.

9. Get up early in the morning is helpful.

10. Eat an apple a day keeps you healthy.

---- **Exercise 1-1** --

다음 주어진 문장을 문법에 맞게 고치세요.

1. I decided meet her again.

2. My dream is be a dentist.

3. He stopped drink because he was thirsty.

4. His hobby is take photos.

5. Swim fast is his aim.

6. I don't expect do it for free.

7. We planned leave this building secretly tonight.

8. I hope meet her as soon as possible.

9. Choose good books is very important for children.

10. Meet her makes me happy.

EXERCISE

다음 문장을 진주어 /가주어 문장으로 바꾸어 쓰세요.

1. To watch three movies a day is so stressful.
=

2. To make a new friend is not easy for her.
=

3. To play too long in the sun is bad for your health.
=

4. To take a stroll with a dog makes you peaceful.
=

5. To meet people like her is not easy.
=

---- **Exercise 2-1** ---

다음 진주어 /가주어 문장을 본래 문장으로 바꾸어 쓰세요.

1. It is fun to play computer games together.
=

2. It was wonderful to meet you in another country.
=

3. It is not easy to keep pets.
=

4. It is very important to follow his instructions.
=

5. It is unhealthy to eat hamburgers every day.
=

---- **Exercise 3** --

주어진 단어를 활용하고 to 부정사를 이용하여 영작하세요.

1. 최선을 다하는 것이 중요하다. (do your best)

→

2. 나는 집에 가서 자기를 원한다.

→

3. 나의 계획은 첫 번째 기차를 타는 것이다. (train, get on)

→

4. 나는 덜 먹을 필요가 있다. (eat less)

→

5. 서로 돕는 것이 필수적이다. (one another, necessary)

→

6. Justin은 살이 빠지기 시작했다. (lose weight)

→

7. 나는 언젠가 그 거리에 가보고 싶다. (hope, visit)

→

---- **Exercise 3-1** --

주어진 단어를 활용하고 to 부정사를 이용하여 영작하세요.

1. 나의 취미는 영화를 보는 것이다. (see)

→

2. 아침에 일찍 일어나는 것은 건강에 좋다. (good for health)

→

3. 나는 내일 그녀를 만나기로 결심했다. (decide)

→

4. 나는 차가운 뭔가를 마시고 싶다. (something cold)

→

5. 가수가 되는 것은 나의 꿈이다. (become)

→

6. 우리는 위험을 감수하기로 결심했다. (take a risk)

→

unit 18 의문사 + to부정사

: '의문사 + to부정사'의 형태를 가지며 to부정사의 명사적 용법과 동일하게
'주어, 목적어, 보어'의 역할을 한다.

what to	무엇을 ~할지
which to	어떤 것을 ~할지
where to	어디에 ~할지
when to	언제 ~할지
how to	어떻게 ~할지, ~하는 방법

- **What to** read **was important to the students.**

  무엇을 읽어야 할지가 그 학생들에게 중요했다.

- **I asked him where to** try on the jacket.

  나는 그에게 어디서 그 재킷을 입어봐야 할지 물었다.

- **I forgot when to** visit the nursing home.

  나는 언제 요양소를 방문해야 할지 잊었다.

- **When to** cancel the concert **is important.**

  언제 콘서트가 취소될지가 중요하다.

- **How to** get my money back **is a question.**

  어떻게 내 돈을 돌려받을지가 의문이다.

EXERCISE

---- **Exercise 1** --

다음 해석에 맞게 빈칸에 알맞은 단어를 써넣으세요.

1. l don't know_____him. (나는 어디서 그를 만나야할지 모른다.)

2. She is wondering_____lasagna. (그녀는 라자냐를 요리하는 방법을 궁금해 하고 있다.)

3. Let me know_____this door. (이 문을 어떻게 여는지 알려주세요.)

4. She doesn't know_____. (그녀는 어디에서 시작해야 할지 모른다.)

5. Do you know_____the violin? (너는 바이올린을 어떻게 켜는지 아니?)

---- **Exercise 1-1** --

다음 해석에 맞게 빈칸에 알맞은 단어를 써넣으세요.

1. They told me_____to the airport.
   그들은 나에게 어떻게 공항에 가야하는지 말해줬다.

2. l asked him _____the game.
   나는 그에게 언제 게임을 시작하는지 물었다.

3. l can't decide_____for lunch.
   나는 점심으로 무엇을 요리해야 하는지 결정할 수 없다.

4. My friend told me_____the level test.
   내 친구는 나에게 언제 레벨테스트가 시작하는지 말해줬다.

5. l know_____ this big watermelon into the small refrigerator.
   나는 이 큰 수박을 어떻게 작은 냉장고에 넣는지 알고 있다.

unit 19 to부정사의 형용사적 용법

: to 부정사는 명사를 수식하는 형용사적 용법을 가진다. to 부정사는 뒤에서 앞으로 수식하며, 주로 '~할'이라고 해석되는 미래적 의미를 가진다.

 to 부정사의 형용사적 용법이 가지는 특징

a. 뒤에서 앞으로 수식

b. 미래적 의미를 가짐

• I have <u>something</u> to tell you.

　나는 너에게 말할 무언가가 있다.

• I bought <u>a hamburger</u> to eat for lunch.

　나는 점심으로 먹을 햄버거 하나를 샀다.

c. 필요한 경우 to부정사 뒤에 전치사를 사용

• I'm looking for a <u>house</u> to live <u>in</u>.

　나는 살 집을 찾고 있다.

• I have no <u>one</u> to talk <u>with</u>.

　나에게는 이야기를 나눌 사람이 없다.

EXERCISE

---- **Exercise 1** --

다음 문장을 문법에 맞게 고친 후 해석하세요.

1. Please, give me something drink.

→

2. She is not a girl say that.

→

3. He wants a pair of pants wear.

→

4. I bought some medicine take during the trip.

→

5. There will be an answer solve this problem.

→

6. This letter has huge power persuade people.

→

7. To be patient is not an easy thing achieve on this trip.

→

---- **Exercise 1-1** --

다음 문장을 문법에 맞게 고친 후 해석하세요.

1. They have lots of homework do tonight.

→

2. I'm hungry. I need something eat.

→

3. Jane bought some books read.

→

4. Seoul is a nice place visit.

→

5. You have nothing lose.

→

6. Andrew bought a car drive.

→

7. Harry bought some medicine improve his health.

→

---- **Exercise 2** ---

다음 괄호 안의 단어들을 적절히 배열하여 문장을 완성하세요.

1. I made (to / a doll / my daughter / give).

→

2. She doesn't have (to / with / write / a pencil).

→

3. Could you give me (sit / a chair / to / on)?

→

4. I am so tired. I am looking for (to / sleep / a bed / in).

→

5. I have (a lot of / do / work / to).

→

---- **Exercise 2-1** ---

다음 괄호 안의 단어들을 적절히 배열하여 문장을 완성하세요.

1. I have (you / show / some pictures / to).

→

2. I have (no friend / with / to / play).

→

3. He brought (to / after / a baby / look).

→

4. She is not (a person / a lie / to / tell).

→

---- **Exercise 3** --

다음 주어진 문장을 영작하세요.

1. 나는 먹을 무언가가 필요하다.

→

2. 나는 그녀를 도와줄 누군가를 알고 있다.

→

3. 제게 앉을 의자 좀 주실 수 있으세요?

→

4. 그녀는 같이 놀 친구들이 없다.

→

5. 그는 읽을 몇 권의 잡지들을 샀다. (magazines)

→

---- **Exercise 3-1** --

다음 주어진 단어를 활용하여 다음 주어진 문장을 영작하세요.

1. 마실 것 좀 드릴까요? (Would you~)

→

2. 그녀는 그렇게 많이 먹을 사람이 아니다.

→

3. 나는 얘기를 나눌 누군가가 필요하다.

→

4. Jack은 살 집을 소유하고 있나요? (own)

→

5. 우리는 해야할 일들이 많다.

→

unit 20 to부정사의 부사적 용법

: 부사는 문장 구성에 영향을 주지 않고 꾸며주는 역할 만을 한다.

따라서 to부정사가 부사적 용법으로 쓰인 경우 문장에서 제거해도 문장이 어색하지 않다.

또한, 부사처럼 명사를 제외한 동사, 형용사, 또 다른 부사, 그리고 문장 전체를 꾸며주는 역할을 한다.

목적: ~하기 위해서

- I do volunteer work to make myself happy.
  나는 내 스스로 행복해지기 위해서 자원봉사를 한다.

- He is going to go to Spain to learn Spanish.
  그는 스페인어를 공부하기 위해 스페인에 갈 예정이다.

- She will go to the sea again to catch fish.
  그녀는 물고기를 잡으러 바다에 다시 갈 것이다.

2 원인: ~하다니, ~해서

: 감정을 나타내는 단어 뒤에 부사적 용법으로 to부정사가 올 수 있는데 이 경우, 뒤에서 앞으로 해석한다.

감정을 나타내는 형용사	sad, happy, nervous, glad, excited, surprised 등

- I was excited to put up a tent all by myself.
  나는 나 혼자서 텐트를 쳐서 신났다.

- She was depressed to gain too much weight.
  그녀는 너무 살쪄서 우울했다.

3 형용사 수식: 뒤에서 앞에 있는 형용사를 수식

- I am lucky to find you here.
  나는 너를 여기서 발견해서 행운이다.

- The mountain is hard to climb.
  그 산은 오르기 힘들다.

- This chapter is difficult to understand.
  이 장은 이해하기 어렵다.

EXERCISE

다음 주어진 문장의 부사적 용법에 유의하여 해석하세요.

1. He planned to go to Australia to meet his friend.

→

2. She called him just to say good-bye.

→

3. I'm really happy to see you again.

→

4. He is so excited to see the movie.

→

5. I sat down on a chair to take a photo.

→

6. We can do anything to help people in need.

→

7. John made a donation of 10,000,000 won to help the flood victims.

→

8. To make a long-term plan is important to succeed.

→

9. I will do my best on this exam to get a scholarship.

→

---- **Exercise 1-1** --

다음 주어진 문장의 부사적 용법에 유의하여 해석하세요.

1. I am so sorry to hear that.

→

2. I went to church to pray for peace.

→

3. She called him to make an apology.

→

4. I was shocked to observe the horrible accident.

→

5. This river is dangerous to swim.

→

6. Jane is going to the library to study hard.

→

7. Susan cleaned the house to please her mother.

→

8. We will go to Paris to visit the Versailles Palace.

→

9. She is happy to study in a group.

→

---- **Exercise 2** --

다음 주어진 문장을 영작하세요.

1. 나는 너를 만나니 반갑다.

→

2. 그녀는 그녀의 엄마를 만나기 위해 왔다.

→

3. 우리는 그 편지를 읽어서 슬퍼졌다.

→

4. 그녀의 삶은 이해하기 어렵다.

→

5. 그는 편지를 쓰기 위해 의자에 앉았다.

→

---- **Exercise 2-1** --

다음 주어진 문장을 영작하세요.

1. 나는 버스를 잡기 위해 달리고 있다. (catch the bus)

→

2. 나는 단지 고맙다고 말하려고 전화했다. (say thanks)

→

3. 나는 돈을 빌리기 위해서 은행에 갔다. (borrow)

→

4. 그는 그 봉투를 받아서 감동했다 (move, envelope).

→

5. 그녀는 어제 우연히 나를 만나서 놀랐다. (surprise, by chance)

→

unit 20 to부정사의 부사적 용법

4 too ~ to / enough to

a. too + 형용사 /부사 + to: 너무 ~해서 ~하지 못하다./ 할 수 없다.

= so~ that 주어 + can't

- The mother was too busy to play with her son.
= The mother was so busy that she couldn't play with her son.
  그 엄마는 너무 바빠서 그녀의 아들과 놀아주지 못했다.
- He is too poor to have three meals.
  그는 너무 가난해서 세끼를 먹지 못한다.

b. 형용사 /부사 + enough to: ~할 만큼 충분히 ~하다.

= so ~that 주어 + can

- She is tall enough to reach the ceiling.
= she is so tall that she can reach the ceiling.
  그녀는 천장에 닿을 만큼 충분히 키가 크다.
- He is strong enough to move the furniture.
  그는 그 가구를 옮길 만큼 충분히 강하다.

EXERCISE

다음 문장을 보기를 참고하여 바꾸세요.

> 보 기
> a. I am so tired that I can't run now.
> = I am too tired to run now.
> b. I am so strong that I can run a marathon.
> = I am strong enough to run a marathon.

1. He is so busy that he cannot call her.

→

2. She is so poor that she cannot buy a car.

→

3. John is so kind that he can understand my son's rudeness.

→

4. Jane is so fat that she can't wear the jeans.

→

5. I am so tall that I can apply for a super model.

→

6. David is too selfish to understand others' feelings.

→

7. They are so brave that they can face the strong enemy.

→

8. The cat is so big that he cannot enter the room.

→

9. Bob got up so late that he couldn't catch the bus.

→

10. She is so busy that she cannot spend time with her boyfriend.

→

---- **Exercise 1-1** ---

다음 문장을 보기를 참고하여 바꾸세요.

보 기
a. I am so tired that I can't run now.
= I am too tired to run now.
b. I am so strong that I can run a marathon.
= I am strong enough to run a marathon.

1. He is so lazy that he cannot get up early in the morning.

→

2. He is so kind that he can drive her home.

→

3. Jane is so weak that she cannot beat John.

→

4. She is so beautiful that she can be famous at school.

→

5. I am so old that I cannot work anymore.

→

6. This problem is so difficult that I cannot solve it.

→

7. We are so tired that we cannot go jogging now.

→

8. I am so lucky that I can join your team.

→

9. This dog is so dirty that we cannot let him in.

→

10. She is so young that she cannot understand others' lives.

→

EXERCISE

다음 주어진 문장을 영작하세요.

1. 나는 너무 어려서 수영할 수 없다. (too)

→

2. 나는 농구를 잘 할 만큼 키가 충분히 크다. (enough)

→

3. 그는 나를 이길 만큼 충분히 강하다. (beat, enough)

→

4. 그녀는 너무 게을러서 일찍 일어날 수 없다. (lazy, too)

→

5. John은 수영할 만큼 충분히 건강하다. (healthy, enough)

→

6. 그는 그 기차를 타기에 충분히 일찍 일어났다. (get on the train, enough)

→

7. 그는 너무 가난해서 방세를 내지 못했다. (pay the rent, too)

→

8. Brian은 그 문제를 이해할 만큼 충분히 똑똑하다. (enough)

→

9. 그는 그 법을 바꿀 만큼 충분히 영향력 있다. (influential, enough)

→

---- **Exercise 2-1** ---

다음 주어진 문장을 영작하세요.

1. 그녀는 그 책을 읽기에 너무 졸리다. (sleepy, too)

→

2. 그는 버스를 따라잡을 만큼 충분히 빠르다. (catch up with, enough)

→

3. 그는 너무 가난해서 그 집을 살 수 없다. (too)

→

4. 그 개는 너무 더러워서 이 건물에 들어오게 할 수 없다. (let in, too)

→

5. 그녀는 그녀의 친구를 도와줄 만큼 충분히 친절하다. (enough)

→

6. 이 중고차는 내 동생에게 주기에 충분히 좋다. (the used car, enough)

→

7. 그는 너무 뚱뚱해서 그 셔츠를 입지 못한다. (the shirt, too)

→

8. 그녀는 정시에 도착할 만큼 충분히 빠르다. (on time, enough)

→

9. Julie는 너무 약해서 이 책상을 옮기지 못한다. (too)

→

: to부정사는 원래는 동사였기 때문에 동사처럼 부정을 표시하거나
자체적으로 주어(의미상 주어)를 가질 수 있다.

1 부정형: to부정사 바로 앞에 not이나 never을 붙여서 부정을 나타낸다.

• I pretended not to be nervous.

나는 긴장하지 않은 척했다.

• She always tries never to be late.

그녀는 항상 절대 늦지 않으려고 노력한다.

2 의미상의 주어

a. of 명사: 사람의 성질을 나타내는 형용사 뒤에서

honest, silly, wise, polite, kind, rude, generous, nice, clever 등

• It was generous of you to share food with the beggar.

네가 그 거지와 음식을 나누어 먹은 것은 관대한 것이었다.

• It is silly of her not to follow the instruction.

그녀가 지시를 따르지 않은 것은 어리석다.

b. for 명사: 그 밖의 형용사

important, possible, impossible, necessary, easy, hard, difficult, essential 등

• For him to stay longer, I lied to my mother.

그가 더 오래 머물게 하기 위해서, 나는 어머니께 거짓말을 했다.

• It is difficult for him to stay focused.

집중하는 것은 그에게 힘들다.

---- **Exercise 1** --

다음 문장을 해석하세요.

1. It was not wise of her to ignore the poor.

→

2. The government set up the policy for all the villagers to preserve the environment.

→

3. I have a great way for you to understand French grammar.

→

4. It was clever of us not to say anything.

→

5. It is hard for me to wait for someone.

→

EXERCISE

다음 문장을 영작하세요.

1. 내가 그 문제를 푸는 것은 쉽다.

→

2. John이 불을 만드는 것은 어렵다. (make fire)

→

3. 나는 그와 말하지 않겠다고 결심했다.

→

4. 내가 그 시험을 통과하는 것은 중요하다. (pass)

→

5. 그가 빨리 달리는 것은 어렵지 않다.

→

---- **Exercise 2-1** --

다음 문장을 영작하세요.

1. 내가 너를 웃게 만드는 건 어렵지 않다.

→

2. 나는 그 사실을 알지 못하는 척 했다.

→

3. 나는 그들이 그것을 이해하는 좋은 방법을 갖고 있다. (have a great way)

→

4. 나는 울지 않으려고 노력했다.

→

5. 이 자전거는 Jane이 타기에 쉽지 않다.

→

[1-4] 밑줄 친 to부정사의 용법을 말하고 해석하세요.

1 It was difficult <u>to understand</u> the problem clearly.

2 <u>To satisfy</u> her, I started to smile often.

3 I made some salad <u>to eat</u> for lunch.

4 My mother really wanted <u>to help</u> me.

5 다음 밑줄 친 부분의 쓰임이 <보기>와 같은 것은?

<보기>
My dream is <u>to be</u> a short-story writer.

① The first goal was <u>to keep</u> a diary every day.
② He went to America <u>to study</u> math.
③ I'm so happy <u>to see</u> you now.
④ I have a lot of novels <u>to read</u>.
⑤ She doesn't have friends <u>to play</u> with.

[6-8] 다음 밑줄 친 부분의 쓰임이 나머지와 <u>다른</u> 하나는?

6
① I'm looking for a chair <u>to sit</u> on.
② He went to America <u>to study</u> math.
③ Do you have something <u>to eat</u>?
④ There are many magazines <u>to read</u>.
⑤ I received the samples <u>to give</u> out.

7
① <u>To leave</u> early today is hard.
② <u>To study</u> math is boring.
③ It is interesting <u>to read</u> novels.
④ Minsoo's goal was <u>to get</u> money.
⑤ <u>To listen</u> to English news is helpful.

8
① It is difficult <u>to say</u> good-bye.
② I don't know <u>how to do</u>.
③ His hobby is <u>to take</u> pictures.
④ She brought some cake <u>to eat</u>.
⑤ <u>To study</u> other languages is not easy.

9 다음 빈칸에 들어갈 말로 바르게 짝지어진 것은?

• She has many friends to play_____.
• You need some paper to write_____.

① with - in
② X - on
③ with - on
④ to - in
⑤ to - X

10 다음 우리말을 영어로 바르게 옮긴 것은? (답2개)

그녀는 너무 어려서 그녀의 이름을 쓸 수 없었다.

① She was too young to write her own name.
② She was young enough to write her own name.
③ She was so young that he could write her own name.
④ She was very young, so she could write her own name.
⑤ She was so young that she couldn't write her own name.

[11-12] 다음 중 어법상 맞는 문장은?

11
① She doesn't know how to use this machine.
② They know how should ride a bicycle.
③ She doesnt't have a pen to write.
④ I want play the guitar.
⑤ It's difficult learn Korean.

12
① To study English is fun.
② I don't have any friends to play.
③ She would like to have a house to live.
④ I need some paper to write.
⑤ I found things to sell to.

[13-15] 밑줄 친 부분이 문장에서 주어, 목적어, 보어 중 어떤 역할을 하는지 쓰세요.

13 Billy is trying to make new friends.
(   )

14 My hobby is to listen to jazz music.
(   )

15 To sleep well is important for your health.
(   )

16 다음 빈칸에 들어갈 단어가 나머지 넷과 다른 것은?

① It is kind_____you to help me.
② It is difficult_____her to get an A.
③ It is important_____me to save money.
④ It is hard_____me to write an essay in French.
⑤ It is necessary_____him to read a lot of books.

[17-18] 다음 밑줄 친 부분의 쓰임이 나머지와 다른 하나를 고르세요.

17
① He prepared some food to take in the park.
② I want to order a hamburger.
③ Minsoo needs a jacket to wear in the morning.
④ I have something to give you.
⑤ She has a lot of work to do today in the office.

18
① I don't have time <u>to watch</u> the drama.
② Do you have any friends <u>to hang out with</u>.
③ I had to hurry <u>to catch</u> the bus.
④ He met a baby <u>to take</u> care of.
⑤ There's nothing <u>to worry</u> about.

19 다음 중 밑줄 친 부분의 쓰임이 같은 것끼리 묶인 것은?

ⓐ <u>To have</u> a good friend, be a good person first.
ⓑ I intend <u>to major</u> in economics next year.
ⓒ I should buy a pen <u>to write</u> with.
ⓓ She is the very first person <u>to help</u>.
ⓔ My father's dream was <u>to be</u> a pilot.

① ⓐ, ⓑ   ② ⓑ, ⓒ
③ ⓑ, ⓓ   ④ ⓒ, ⓓ
⑤ ⓓ, ⓔ

[20-21] 다음 괄호 안의 단어를 알맞은 형태로 바꿔 빈칸에 쓰세요.

20

I need a coat_____in winter. (wear)

21

She came early_____fresh meat. (buy)

22 다음 빈칸에 들어갈 말로 알맞은 것은?

A: Do you have any hobbies?
B: Not really. How about you?
A: My hobby is_____stamps.

① collection
② collect
③ collected
④ to collect
⑤ to collecting

[23-24] 다음 대화를 읽고, 물음에 답하세요.

A: What's up, Hyo?
B: I failed my English exam.
   I really don't know ①무엇을 해야 할지.
A: Don't take it so hard. How about studying
   with me tonight?
B: Thank you, Hyo. It's very kind ②_____
to offer to help me.

23 위 글의 ①에 주어진 한글과 의미가 통하도록 영작하세요.

→ _____.

24 위 글의 ②에 들어갈 말로 알맞은 것은?

① your
② to you
③ for you
④ of you
⑤ in you

Chapter 5 to부정사

25 다음 두 문장을 to 부정사를 사용하여 한 문장
으로 고쳐 쓰세요.

(1)

He wants to buy a big house.
He will live in the house.

→ He wants_____a big house

_____.

(2)

Sojin needs a chair. She will sit on the
chair.

→ Sojin needs_____.

6 동명사와 분사
Chapter

Gorilla Grammar

unit 22 동명사의 명사적 용법

: 동명사는 동사에 ing를 붙여 명사의 역할을 한다. 따라서 명사처럼 주어, 목적어, 보어자리에 들어갈 수 있다. to부정사의 명사적 역할과 역할이 겹친다.

다만, 주어와 보어 자리에는 동명사와 to부정사 둘 다 사용가능하나 목적어 자리에 동명사가 올지 to부정사가 올지는 동사에 달려있다.

a. 주어 역할

- **Relaxing** after an exam is necessary. (= To relax after an exam is necessary.)

  시험 후에 쉬는 것은 필수적이다.

- **Having** a surprise party is our plan. (= To have a surprise party is our plan.)

  깜짝 파티를 여는 것이 우리의 계획이다.

b. 보어 역할

- His plan is **getting** closer to the man. (= His plan is to get closer to the man.)

  그의 계획은 그 남자에게 접근하는 것이다.

- Her aim is **taking** a picture of the famous actor.

  (= Her aim is to take a picture of the famous actor.)

  그녀의 목표는 그 유명한 배우의 사진을 찍는 것이다.

c. 목적어 역할

- She denied **being** on a business trip.

  그녀는 출장 중인 것을 부인했다.

- I enjoy **catching** fish.

  나는 물고기를 잡는 것을 즐긴다.

---- **Exercise 1** --

다음 밑줄 친 동명사의 역할을 쓰세요. (주어/보어/목적어)

1. <u>Playing</u> the guitar is fun.

→

2. We enjoy <u>swimming.</u>

→

3. My hobby is <u>taking</u> a nap.

→

4. When did you quit <u>smoking</u>?

→

5. My plan is <u>traveling</u> all around the world.

→

6. She tried <u>doing</u> that.

→

7. I remember <u>meeting</u> you.

→

8. <u>Listening</u> to the music is helpful for me to reduce daily stress.

→

EXERCISE

---- **Exercise 1-1** ---

다음 밑줄 친 동명사의 역할을 쓰세요. (주어/보어/목적어)

1. Preparing a surprise party is my mission.

→

2. It began raining this morning.

→

3. Would you mind opening the window?

→

4. Living alone is being free from care.

→

5. Swimming makes you feel alive.

→

6. My plan is buying a big house.

→

7. Eating local food is the fun part of my journey.

→

8. The important thing is doing your best.

→

---- **Exercise 2** ---

다음 문장을 동명사를 활용하여 영작하세요.

1. 네 삶에서 중요한 것은 사람들을 사랑하는 것이다.

→

2. 다른 사람을 이해하는 것은 쉽지 않다.

→

3. 나는 그 바에서 술마시는 것을 즐긴다. (at the bar)

→

4. 사람들과 이야기를 나누는 것은 나의 행복이다.

→

5. 그는 그녀를 괴롭히는 것을 그만뒀다. (quit, bother)

→

unit 23 동명사와 to부정사의 비교

: 동명사와 to부정사는 둘 다 명사적 역할을 한다는 데에 역할이 겹친다. 따라서 둘 다 주어, 목적어, 보어자리에 들어갈 수 있는데 주어와 보어자리에는 둘 중 아무거나 써도 괜찮지만 목적어자리에는 동사에 따라 to부정사가 올지, 동명사가 올지 결정되니 조심해야한다.

1 주어

- To learn about foreign culture is fun.
= Learning about foreign culture is fun.
외국 문화를 배우는 것은 재미있다.
- To follow the rules is important.
= Following the rules is important.
그 규칙들을 따르는 것은 중요하다.

2 보어

- My hobby is to collect stamps.
= My hobby is collecting stamps.
나의 취미는 우표를 모으는 것이다.
- His plan is to learn computers.
= His plan is learning computers.
그의 계획은 컴퓨터를 배우는 것이다.

3 목적어

a. to 부정사를 목적어로 받는 동사

want, plan, decide, pretend, expect, learn, hope 등

- I <u>decided</u> to share happiness with him.
  나는 그와 행복을 공유하기로 결심했다.
- She <u>wants</u> to take a lesson.
  그녀는 수업을 듣길 원한다.

b. 동명사를 목적어로 받는 동사

enjoy, imagine, consider, allow 등

- They <u>enjoyed</u> making plans.
  그들은 계획을 세우는 것을 즐겼다.
- She <u>imagined</u> calling him Prince.
  그녀는 그를 왕자님이라고 부르는 것을 상상했다.

c. 둘 다 목적어로 받을 수 있는 동사

start, begin, love, like, hate 등

- I <u>started</u> to run toward them.
- = I <u>started</u> running toward them.
  나는 그들을 향해 달리기 시작했다.
- I <u>like</u> to take my pet for a walk.
- = I <u>like</u> taking my pet for a walk.
  나는 내 애완동물을 산책시키는 것을 좋아한다.

d. 목적어에 따라 의미가 달라지는 동사

remember to부정사	~할 것을 기억한다. (미래)
remember ~ing	~했던 것을 기억한다. (과거)

forget to부정사	~할 것을 잊다. (미래)
forget ~ing	~했던 것을 잊다. (과거)

stop to부정사	~하기 위해서 멈추다.
stop ~ing	~하는 것을 멈추다.

- You should <u>remember</u> to get up early tomorrow.
  너는 내일 일찍 일어나야 할 것을 기억해야한다.

- I <u>remember</u> getting up early yesterday.
  나는 어제 일찍 일어났던 것을 기억한다.

- What if he <u>forgets</u> to bring the document?
  그가 그 서류를 가져올 것을 잊으면 어쩌지?

- He <u>forgot</u> having a good time with her.
  그는 그녀와 즐거운 시간을 보냈다는 것을 잊었다.

- He <u>stopped</u> to call her.
  그는 그녀에게 전화걸기 위해 멈췄다.

- He <u>decided</u> to stop calling her.
  그는 그녀에게 전화 거는 것을 그만두기로 결심했다.

---- **Exercise 1** --

다음 문장 중 틀린 부분을 고치세요. (정답 여러 개 가능)

1. My dream is will be a doctor.

→

2. I decided studying English hard.

→

3. To speaking Korean is not that easy.

→

4. Would you mind to open the window?

→

5. Don't give up to read this book.

→

6. I want being a singer.

→

7. The baby began to crying.

→

8. Do you hope meeting me again?

→

9. I remember to say it to you yesterday.

→

10. She forgot meeting him next week.

→

EXERCISE

---- **Exercise 2** --

다음 주어진 문장을 to부정사 또는 동명사를 활용해서 영작하세요.

1. 그는 농구하기를 원한다.

→

2. 그녀는 영어로 쓰는 것을 배웠다.

→

3. 중요한 것은 친구들을 사랑하는 것이다.

→

4. 너와 함께한다는 것은 나의 기쁨이다. (pleasure)

→

5. 나는 그에게 문을 닫으라고 말했다.

→

6. 보는 것이 믿는 것이다.

→

7. 나의 취미는 그림을 그리는 것이다.

→

8. 나는 그를 그리는 것을 포기했다.

→

9. 나는 너를 다시 보기를 희망한다.

→

10. 나는 네가 집으로 돌아오기를 원한다.

→

Junior Gorilla Grammar   Level 2

---- **Exercise 2-1** ---

다음 주어진 문장을 to부정사 또는 동명사를 활용해서 영작하세요.

1. 우리는 쇼핑하러 가기로 결정했다.

→

2. 나는 치과의사가 되고 싶다. (a dentist)

→

3. 나는 담배를 피우기 위해 멈췄다.

→

4. 나는 담배 피우는 것을 멈췄다. (금연했다)

→

5. 그는 다시는 담배를 피우지 않기로 약속했다. (promise, stop)

→

6. 우리는 싸우기를 멈췄다. (fight)

→

7. 그들은 싸우기 위해 멈췄다.

→

8. 너는 그녀를 만났던 것을 잊었다.

→

9. 너는 내일 그녀를 만날 것을 기억해야 한다. (should)

→

10. 그는 책을 훔쳤다는 것을 부인했다. (deny, steal)

→

unit 24 분사의 형용사적 용법

: 분사는 형용사역할을 하므로 명사를 꾸며준다. 단독으로 꾸밀 때는 형용사처럼 앞에서 뒤로 꾸미고 길어질 경우 뒤에서 앞으로 꾸민다.

분사	현재분사	동사 + ing → 능동의 뜻
	과거분사	동사의 p. p. 형 → 수동의 뜻

1 현재분사

- a **shouting** boy

  소리 지르는 소년

- a boy **shouting** at the mirror

  거울에 대고 소리 지르는 소년

2 과거분사

- a **recommended** lecture

  추천되는 강의

- a lecture **recommended** by the teacher

  그 선생님에 의해서 추천되는 강의

---- **Exercise 1** --

다음 괄호 안에 적절한 형태에 O표 하세요.

1. The (dancing / danced) girls look like angels.

2. I bought a (using / used) bike because of the money problem.

3. I read a novel (written / writing) in English.

4. We saw a (slept / sleeping) baby in the bathroom.

5. This computer game is very (excited / exciting).

6. The building (building / built) here will be sold to him.

7. The meat (cooked / cooking) by him is still not served.

8. The movie was so (touched / touching), so I was very (moved / moving).

9. He is (surprised / surprising) at the (surprised / surprising) result.

EXERCISE

다음 괄호 안에 적절한 형태에 O표 하세요.

1. There are some (cried / crying) babies in the (broken / breaking) house.

2. I met a girl (named / naming) Sally yesterday.

3. Look at the man (sleeping / slept) under the tree.

4. They shot the bird (flying / flied) in the sky.

5. When are you going to fix the (broke / broken / breaking) door?

6. (Used / Using) papers and cans should be placed in the (recycling / recycled) bin.

7. You may be faced with (unexpecting / unexpected) danger.

8. I am tired of eating (boiled / boiling) eggs.

9. I saw Jane (cooked / cooking) in the kitchen.

10. I've never seen a whale (caught / catching) in the river.

[1-2] 빈칸에 들어갈 알맞은 것을 고르세요.

1

> _____regularly is a good habit.

① Work out
② Works out
③ Worked out
④ Working out
⑤ Being worked out

2

> John is very interested in_____
> foreign languages.

① learn
② learns
③ learned
④ to learn
⑤ learning

3 나음 중 밑줄 친 부분의 쓰임이 살못된 것은?

① Would you mind <u>to take</u> off your coat?
② I stopped <u>drinking</u> Coke a month ago.
③ I enjoyed <u>playing</u> online games yesterday.
④ She decided <u>to apply</u> for the job.
⑤ Her wish is <u>to live</u> with her baby.

4 다음 중 밑줄 친 부분의 쓰임이 <u>잘못된</u> 것은?

① They will attempt <u>to rescue</u> the victims.
② She put off <u>to send</u> him money.
③ They agreed <u>to sing</u> a song.
④ He hopes <u>to go</u> on a vacation soon.
⑤ Because she was nervous, she refused <u>to speak</u> in front of them.

5 다음 중 밑줄 친 동사를 바르게 고친 것은?

> In many English dictionaries <u>publish</u> lately,
> we can find a number of new words.

① have been published
② publish
③ published
④ publishing
⑤ are publishing

[6-7] 빈칸을 주어진 단어의 형태를 적절히 바꿔서
채우세요.

6 A boy_____at her is her brother. (yell)

7 The girl_____Minji is very pretty.
(name)

[8-10] 괄호 안에 주어진 말 중 알맞은 것을 고르세요.

8

> He promised (to pay / paying) back the
> money within a month.

9

> Harry kindly agreed (to help / helping) me
> find a good doctor.

10

> I never expected (seeing / to see) her
> again.

11 다음 중 빈칸에 들어갈 수 없는 것은?

> My sister_____talking about her golf
> lesson.

① avoided
② continued
③ began
④ wanted
⑤ stopped

12 다음 중 밑줄 친 용법이 나머지 넷과 다른 것은?

① My hobby is <u>collecting</u> foreign stamps.
② My dream is <u>coming</u> true right now.
③ His goal is <u>scoring</u> A in math.
④ Her wish is <u>having</u> a baby of her own.
⑤ My concern is <u>being</u> back at work soon.

13 다음 중 밑줄 친 용법이 나머지 넷과 다른 것은?

① I tried to chase the <u>running</u> dog.
② I enjoyed <u>singing</u> with you.
③ <u>Studying</u> at night makes me tired.
④ They denied <u>calling</u> names.
⑤ <u>Having</u> three meals a day can keep you healthy.

14 다음 중 밑줄 친 부분의 쓰임이 잘못된 것은?

① The <u>barked</u> dog tried to bite me.
② The boy <u>refused</u> by her didn't want to go out.
③ I'm interested in <u>joining</u> the club.
④ The man <u>lying</u> on the couch is about to fall
asleep.
⑤ The <u>smiling</u> girl looks attractive.

15 다음 문장에서 틀린 곳을 찾아 바르게 고치세요.

> When the boy saw the slept lion, he hid behind the wall.

_____ → _____

16 빈 칸에 들어갈 말로 알맞은 것은?

> I approached a man_____ in front of the door.

① stood
② to standing
③ to be stood
④ standing
⑤ stand

17 다음 대화의 빈칸을 주어진 단어를 활용해서 채우세요.

> A: Can we stop_____ some water? (drink)
> B: Sure! I am thirsty, too.

18 다음 대화의 밑줄 친 부분 중 어법상 틀린 것은?

> A: What did you ①do ②last weekend?
> B: I ③really ④enjoyed ⑤to swim in the river.

19 다음 밑줄 친 부분 중 어색한 것은?

> My mother's hobby is ①gardening. She loves ②to grow roses and tulips in her garden. I often ③to help take care of them. She really likes ④to talk about the garden with me. It seems ⑤to be her precious place.

20 다음 밑줄 친 부분 중 to부정사로 바꿔 쓸 수 없는 것은?

① My favorite activity is <u>singing</u> songs.
② <u>Eating</u> candies every day is bad for your teeth.
③ Rabbits like <u>eating</u> grass.
④ It began <u>raining</u> heavily.
⑤ Thank you for <u>sending</u> me nice cookies.

21 다음 밑줄 친 단어를 -ing형으로 바꿀 필요가 없는 것은?

① <u>Travel</u> by train is great fun.
② I'm sorry <u>to hear</u> that.
③ Jinsoo is very good at <u>speak</u> English.
④ <u>Go</u> to bed early is good for you.
⑤ Instead of <u>go</u> shopping, let's go hiking.

Chapter 6 동명사와 분사

22 위 글의 밑줄 친 부분 중 어법상 어색한 것은?

①Meet someone from another culture might ②make you feel strange, too. For example, in Korea, people ③take off their shoes at home. But ④in most western countries, people don't ⑤take off their shoes.

23 다음 주어진 말을 사용하여 빈칸에 알맞은 말을 쓰세요.

I like_____riddles, so I enjoy_____ detective books. (solve, read)

[24-25] 다음 대화를 읽고, 물음에 답하세요.

A: Good morning, Dad.
B: Good morning. Are you ready for breakfast?
A: No. I'm busy ①_____for school.
B: But you need to eat something. ②Start every morning with breakfast is very important.
A: I don't have any appetite.
B: Then, how about ③_____some scrambled eggs and fruit?

24 위 글의 ①과 ③에 들어갈 말로 바르게 짝지어진 것은?

① prepare - eat
② prepare - to eat
③ prepare - eating
④ preparing - eaten
⑤ preparing - eating

25 위 글의 ②를 문법에 맞는 문장으로 다시 쓰세요.

→ _____.

7 등위접속사

Chapter

Gorilla Grammar

: 등위접속사는 단어와 단어, 구와 구, 절과 절을 연결한다. 동등한 관계로 연결이 되었는지 확인하는 것이 가장 중요하다.

접속사	뜻
and	그리고
or	또는
but	그러나
so	그래서
,for	왜냐하면

- He is kind and handsome. (단어와 단어를 연결)

  그는 친절하고 잘생겼다.

- He has a car, and she has a bicycle. (문장과 문장을 연결)

  그는 차를 가지고 있고, 그녀는자전거를 가지고 있다

- She can leave or stay.

  그녀는 떠나거나 머물 수 있다.

- I was very sick, but I went to school.

  나는 매우 아팠다 그러나 나는 학교에 갔다.

- I was very sick, so I didn't go to school.

  나는 매우 아팠다 그래서 나는 학교에 가지 않았다.

- I didn't go to school, for I was very sick.

  나는 학교에 가지 않았다, 왜냐하면 매우 아팠기 때문이다.

■ 명령문 + and /명령문 + or

명령문 + and	~해라, 그러면 ~ 할 것이다
명령문 + or	~해라, 그렇지 않으면 ~ 할 것이다

- Meet her, and you'll get a chance to be a singer.

  그녀를 만나라, 그러면 가수가 될 기회를 얻을 것이다.

- Go to bed right now, or you'll get up late tomorrow.

  일찍 자라, 그렇지 않으면 내일 늦게 일어날 것이다.

---- **Exercise 1** --

다음 괄호 안에 적절한 접속사를 써 넣으세요.

1. I was surprised, (   ) everyone was crying in the house.

2. I came back home (   ) went to bed.

3. He is kind to me, (   ) I don't like him.

4. Which do you prefer, meat (   ) fish?

5. She talks too much, (   ) no one likes her.

6. She will come back tonight (   ) tomorrow.

7. He won the game, (   ) he felt happy.

8. He won the game, (   ) he didn't feel happy.

EXERCISE

---- **Exercise 1-1** --

다음 괄호 안에 적절한 접속사를 써 넣으세요.

1. It was raining outside, (   ) I closed the window.

2. John plays the piano, (   ) his brother doesn't play the piano.

3. John studied hard, (   ) he passed the exam.

4. Would you like to eat (   ) drink?

5. John ate a lot, (   ) he is still hungry.

6. Sally is tall enough, (   ) Susan is much taller.

7. Tom sent a love letter to Sally, (   ) she didn't reply yet.

8. I am so tired, (   ) I didn't sleep well last night.

---- **Exercise 2** --

다음 주어진 문장을 해석하세요.

1. We decided to save money and buy the house.

→

2. They enjoy drinking beer and chattering to each other.

→

3. To love and to be loved is the greatest happiness in life.

→

4. Language is the basis for all knowledge and for all power.

→

5. It is not possible to do it all or to have it all.

→

6. Could you give me something cool, something delicious, and something expensive?

→

EXERCISE

---- **Exercise 2-1** --

다음 주어진 문장을 해석하세요.

1. Would it be better to buy or to rent?

→

2. Why don't you drink a lot of milk and exercise regularly?

→

3. Getting up early makes you feel fresh and gives you a healthy life.

→

4. My goal is to be generous, to be ambitious, and to be a rich man.

→

5. They developed new products made from rice and sold them for a reasonable price.

→

---- **Exercise 3** --

다음 문장을 and/or/but 을 이용하여 영작하세요.

1. 엄마께서는 나에게 집과 차를 사주셨다.

→

2. 너는 여름과 겨울 중에 어느 것을 더 좋아하니? (between)

→

3. 나는 도서관에 갔고, 역사를 공부했다. (library)

→

4. 그녀는 예쁘지만, 성격이 괴팍하다. (bad-tempered)

→

5. 너는 농담을 하고 있는 거겠지, 아니면 제정신이 아니거나. (kidding, crazy)

→

---- **Exercise 3-1** --

다음 문장을 and/or/but 을 이용하여 영작하세요.

1. 엄마께서는 나에게 빵과 우유를 사주셨다. (some)

→

2. 그는 수영을 좋아하지만 바다를 싫어한다.

→

3. 너는 버스나 택시를 탈 수 있디. (take)

→

4. 그는 열심히 공부해서 기말고사에서 좋은 성적을 거두었다. (the final test)

→

5. Tom은 Itaewon에 살고, 근처에서 일한다. (around there)

→

unit 26 등위상관접속사와 병렬

등위상관접속사	해석	수일치
both A and B	A와 B 둘 다	항상 복수취급
either A or B	A와 B 둘 중 하나	B에 일치
neither A nor B	A와 B 둘 다 아닌	B에 일치
not only A but (also) B	A 뿐만 아니라 B도	B에 일치
B as well as A	A 뿐만 아니라 B도	B에 일치
not A but B	A가 아니라 B	B에 일치

• Both John and Jessy want to go to the zoo.

John과 Jessy 둘 다 동물원에 가기를 원한다.

• Either he or I have to stay with her.

그와 나 중에 하나는 그녀와 함께 머물러야만 한다.

• Neither Mindy nor you study hard.

Mindy나 너나 둘 다 공부를 열심히 하지 않는다.

• Not only he but also you are responsible for the crime.

= You as well as he are responsible for the crime.

그 뿐만 아니라 너도 그 범죄에 책임이 있다.

• Not being a student but a worker means a lot to me.

학생이 아니라 일꾼이 된다는 것이 나에게 큰 의미가 있다.

---- **Exercise 1** ---

다음 문장을 보기와 같이 고치세요.

보 기
I hate not only math but also science.
→ I hate science as well as math.

1. He has not only health problems but also money problems.

→

2. Not only Jane but also Tom can swim well.

→

3. Tom bought her not only a car but also a house.

→

4. Not only Samung but also LQ is in debt.

→

5. We play not only soccer but also baseball together.

→

EXERCISE

다음 문장을 보기와 같이 고치세요.

> 보 기
> I like math as well as science.
> → I like not only science but also math.

1. Sally as well as her dog came back to the house.

→

2. I want to own this book as well as read it.

→

3. This rule applies to parents as well as children.

→

4. We are eating rice as well as noodles.

→

5. She is beautiful as well as brave.

→

---- **Exercise 2** --

다음 주어진 문장을 영작하세요. (2가지)

1. 그는 용감할 뿐만 아니라 정직하다.

→

→

2. 내 친구들 뿐만 아니라 나도 수영을 잘 한다.

→

→

3. 그들은 고기 뿐만 아니라 생선도 좋아한다.

→

→

4. 그녀는 아름다울 뿐만 아니라 부자다.

→

→

5. 이 제품은 가격 뿐만 아니라 품질에서도 최고다. (product, the best, in price)

→

→

EXERCISE

다음 문장을 영작하세요. (2가지)

1. 그는 키가 클 뿐 아니라 잘 생겼다.

→

→

2. John은 음악을 듣는 것 뿐 아니라 노래 부르는 것도 좋아한다.

→

→

3. 그들 뿐만 아니라 나도 이 파티에 초대 받았다.

→

→

4. 이것은 살 수 있을 뿐만 아니라 팔수도 있다.

→

→

5. 나는 수박 뿐만 아니라 오렌지도 좋아한다.

→

→

Chapter 7 등위접속사

1 다음 빈칸에 들어갈 말로 바르게 짝지어진 것은?

> A: I don't like candy_____chocolate.
>   What about you?
> B: I don't like candy, _____I like bubble gum.

① and - and
② and - but
③ but - or
④ or - and
⑤ but - and

2 다음 빈칸에 들어갈 말로 알맞은 것을 고르세요.

> I had to move some heavy books,_____
> I asked my friend to move them.

① because   ② so
③ but   ④ if
⑤ though

3 다음 밑줄 친 부분이 의미상 적절하지 <u>않은</u> 것은?

① Get up early, <u>or</u> you will be late.
② Turn to the right, <u>and</u> you'll find the office.
③ Do your best, <u>and</u> you can be a winner.
④ Exercise every day, <u>or</u> you'll be healthy.
⑤ Study hard, <u>and</u> you can speak French well.

[4-5] 다음 문장을 우리말로 바르게 옮긴 것을 고르세요.

4

> She is not a singer but a painter.

① 그녀는 가수도 화가도 아니다.
② 그녀는 화가가 아니라 가수다.
③ 그녀는 가수가 아니라 화가다.
④ 그녀는 가수이자 동시에 화가다.
⑤ 그녀는 가수 또는 화가 둘 중 하나이다.

5

> Hurry up, and you'll be on time.

① 서두르더라도 너는 늦을 것이다.
② 서두르지 않으면 너는 늦을 것이다.
③ 서두르지 않으면 너는 늦을지도 모른다.
④ 서두르면 너는 제시간에 도착할 것이다.
⑤ 서두르면 너는 제시간에 도착할지도 모른다.

6 다음 빈칸에 공통으로 들어갈 말로 알맞은 것은?

> • Consider your talents_____your interests when you choose a career.
> • He was kind_____nice.

① as much as
② as many as
③ as well as
④ as good as
⑤ as ages as

7 다음 중 밑줄 친 부분이 어법상 <u>틀린</u> 것을 고르세요.

> A: ① <u>What</u> do you ② <u>have</u> ③ <u>in</u>
> your plastic bag?
> B: I have two ④ <u>things</u>, a pen ⑤ <u>or</u> a
> mirror.

8 다음 두 문장을 한 문장으로 고쳐 쓸 때 빈칸에 알맞은 말을 쓰세요.

> • He is bored with movie, and he is also
> bored with music.
> → He is bored not only with movie _____
> _____ with music.

9 다음 대화의 빈칸에 들어갈 말로 알맞은 것은?

> A: Dad, I want to play the piano.
> B: No. Go to bed now,_____ you
> will sleep in late tomorrow.

① and   ② or
③ if   ④ unless
⑤ neither

10 다음 빈칸에 들어갈 말이 순서대로 짝지어진 것은?

> • Don't worry,_____ you will make your
> dream come true someday.
> • Clean your room,_____ you won't be
> able to focus on your study.
> • Don't eat heavy dinner,_____ you will
> be healthier.

① and – and – and
② and – and – or
③ and – or – and
④ or – and – or
⑤ or – or – and

[11-12] 다음 빈칸에 들어갈 말로 알맞은 것을 고르세요.

11

> I want to have_____a coat and a watch.

① either   ② neither
③ both   ④ not
⑤ if

12

> Leave home an hour earlier,_____you
> will miss the bus.

① and   ② or
③ if   ④ unless
⑤ neither

13 다음 빈칸에 들어갈 말이 나머지와 <u>다른</u> 하나는?

① Protect flowers,_____honeybees will lose their work.
② Go home by seven o' clock,_____your dad will be angry.
③ Eat breakfast,_____you cannot stay healthy.
④ Look at the sky at night,_____you can see stars.
⑤ Clean your desk,_____you will trip on a stuff and fall down.

14 다음 밑줄 친 부분이 어법상 <u>틀린</u> 것은?

① Both you and I <u>are</u> going to the party.
② Either Min or I <u>am</u> able to get it.
③ Not only Soo but also Min <u>are</u> smart.
④ Neither my mom nor my dad <u>cooks</u> a lot.
⑤ Not my sister but my brother <u>is</u> a teacher.

15 다음 두 문장이 같은 뜻이 되도록 할 때 빈칸에 들어갈 말로 알맞은 것은?

• Not only Min but Soo likes the cake.
= Soo _____ Min likes the cake.

① both   ② either
③ neither   ④ as well
⑤ as well as

16 다음 빈칸에 공통으로 들어갈 말로 알맞은 것은?

• Not only you_____also I saw the scene.
• The girl is not my sister_____Min's.

① both   ② and
③ as   ④ but
⑤ or

17 다음 밑줄 친 부분 중 어법상 <u>틀린</u> 것은?

① <u>Neither</u> I ② <u>or</u> Soo ③ <u>got</u> a ④ <u>message</u>
⑤ <u>from</u> Jimin. (나도 수도 지민에게 메시지를받지 못했다.)

18. 다음 빈칸에 들어갈 말로 알맞은 것은?

Not only my mother but also my father____ to cook Korean dishes.

① like   ② likes
③ is liking   ④ are liking
⑤ have to like

8 Chapter 종속접속사

Gorilla Grammar

unit 27 명사절을 이끄는 접속사

: 명사절을 이끄는 접속사 that, what 뒤에 절이 나오고 그것을 하나의 명사로 취급하여 명사처럼 주어, 목적어, 보어의 역할을 한다.

1 that과 what

명사절 접속사	해석	특징
that	~하는 것	뒤에 완전한 절
what	~하는 것	뒤에 불완전한 절

a. 주어

- That he is a good listener is certain.

  그가 좋은 청자라는 것이 확실하다.

- What I persuaded him to do was an apology. (do의 목적어 없는 불완전절)

  내가 그가 하도록 설득한 것은 사과였다.

- -

★ to부정사와 마찬가지로 명사절도 진주어/가주어 문장으로 바꿀 수 있다. 즉,

- That he is a good listener is certain.
- = It is certain that he is a good listener.

- What I persuaded him to do was an apology.
- = It was an apology what I persuaded him to do.

b. 목적어

- I think that this is a jar.

  나는 이것이 병이라고 생각한다.

- I don't know what you mean.

  나는 네가 의미하는 것을 모르겠다.

★ hope, think, know, believe 등이 동사로 올 때 목적어를 이끄는 명사절 that은
생략이 가능하다.

• I think (that) this is a jar.
  내 생각에 이것은 병이다.

• I know (that) you should change your personality.
  나는 네가 너의 성격을 바꿔야만 한다는 것을 안다.

c. 보어

• My opinion is that I'm for uniforms.
  나의 의견은 교복에 찬성한다는 것이다.

• My dream is what can't come true.
  나의 꿈은 이루어질 수 없는 것이다.

---- **Exercise 1** --

주어진 두 개의 접속사 중에서 올바른 것을 고르세요.

(주어)

1. (That / What) he got a new girlfriend made me jealous.

2. (That / What) bothers her is a fly.

(보어)

1. One of my wishes is (that / what) there will be no war in the world.

2. The answer is (that /what) she decided.

(목적어)

1. I represented (what /that) we needed their help.

2. I bought her (what /that) she really wanted to have.

 if /whether

명사절 접속사	해석	특징
if	~인지 아닌지	뒤에 완전절, 목적어절에만 사용
whether	~인지 아닌지	뒤에 완전절

- Whether she is pretty or not is none of my business. (주어 역할)

  그녀가 예쁜지 안 예쁜지는 나랑 상관없는 일이다.

- My concern is whether he is upset. (보어 역할)

  나의 걱정은 그가 화났는지 아닌지 이다.

- I don't know if /whether I'm interested in math. (목적어 역할)

  나는 내가 수학에 흥미가 있는지 없는지 모르겠다.

---- **Exercise 1-1** --

주어진 두 개의 접속사 중에서 올바른 것을 고르세요.

(주어)

1. (What / That) I got a C on my math test is not surprising.

2. (What / Whether) she likes it or not is unclear to me.

(보어)

1. The goal of this team is (what / that) the district will become clean.

2. The good quality of the product is (what / that) satisfied the customer.

(목적어)

1. I don't know (what / whether) his testimony is true or not.

2. Please, tell me (what / that) you are just OK.

 의문사절

의문 대명사	의문 형용사	의문 부사
who (누가, 누구를)	whose (누구의)	when (언제)
which (어느 것)	which (어느~)	where (어디)
what (무엇)	what (어떤)	why (왜)
		how (얼마나, 어떻게)

★ 명사절의 접속사에서 의문사절은 간접의문문이라는 이름으로도 배운다.

• I know which color you will choose. (의문 형용사) (목적어)
나는 어떤 색깔을 네가 선택할지를 안다.

• My choice depends on what you need. (의문 대명사) (전치사 뒤)
나의 선택은 네가 무엇을 필요로 하는지에 달려있다.

• What genre of movies he likes is my concern. (의문 형용사) (주어)

어떤 장르의 영화를 그가 좋아하는 지가 나의 관심이다.

• I try to appreciate what I have. (~것) (목적어)

나는 내가 가진 것을 감사하려고 노력한다.

• Why she loves me is a question. (의문 부사) (주어)

왜 그녀가 나를 사랑하는 지가 의문이다.

---- **Exercise 1-2** --

주어진 두 개의 접속사 중에서 올바른 것을 고르세요.

(주어)

1. (What /When) I met him is important to them.

2. (How /What) long I have met him is important to them.

(보어)

1. The point is (how / what) much it will cost.

2. His question was (what / when) Insu had met her.

(목적어)

1. I told him (whose / how) book this is.

2. My expression showed (that / what) I really wanted.

---- **Exercise 1-3** --

주어진 두 개의 접속사 중에서 올바른 것을 고르세요.

(주어)

1. (What / Who) will become President depends on our choice.

2. (Where / Which) color he chooses can change the rule.

(보어)

1. The problem is (what / where) he lives.

2. The result depends on (which / why) option they click.

(목적어)

1. My daughter was wondering (that / why) the sky is blue.

2. I know (what / how) he got interested in math.

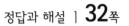
Exercise 1

괄호 안에 알맞은 표현을 고르고 해석하세요.

1. He never tells me (what /that) I want to hear from him.
→

2. (Whether /If) she can speak Korean is uncertain.
→

3. (That /Whether) your father is rich or not is not important.
→

4. I wonder (why /what) he can swim well.
→

5. This is (that /what) he wants to have.
→

6. She doesn't believe (that /why) I am a liar.
→

7. I think (that /when) this is a spoon.
→

8. (What /How) I have lived my life can affect his choice.
→

9. That is (what /that) I mean to do.
→

10. Let me know (what /whether) you are able to join the party.
→

Exercise 2

다음 밑줄 친 명사절이 문장에서 어떤 역할을 하는지 쓰고 해석하세요.

1. The question is <u>why he said that.</u>

2. I believe <u>that I can fly.</u>

3. <u>Whether you can swim or not</u> is not the problem.

4. I wonder <u>if she will come back on time.</u>

5. The problem is <u>that I don't have a car.</u>

Exercise 2-1

다음 밑줄 친 명사절이 문장에서 어떤 역할을 하는지 쓰고 해석하세요.

1. Let me know <u>if you are ready.</u>

2. <u>Whether he loves her</u> is not certain.

3. I think <u>that this is an apple.</u>

4. It is not certain <u>that he is honest.</u>

5. His dream is <u>that he will be able to do something for the peace of the world.</u>

Exercise 3

다음 주어진 문장을 적절한 접속사를 써서 영작하세요.

1. 나의 의견은 나는 그 규칙에 반대한다는 것이다. (object to)

→

2. 나는 네가 무엇을 갖고 싶어 하는지 모른다.

→

3. 네가 곧 20살이 된다는 것은 참 놀랍다. (surprising)

→

4. 그들이 무엇에 관해 이야기하고 있는지 당신은 추측할 수 있나요? (guess, talk about)

→

5. 나는 내가 그녀를 만난 적이 있는지 없는지 기억할 수 없다. (remember, whether)

→

Exercise 3-1

다음 주어진 문장을 적절한 접속사를 써서 영작하세요.

1. 나는 그가 친절하다고 생각한다. (guess)

→

2. 그녀가 영어를 잘 한다는 것은 확실하다. (be good at, certain)

→

3. 나는 너의 꿈이 실현되기를 바란다. (come true)

→

4. 문제는 우리는 서로를 모른다는 것이다. (the problem)

→

5. 그녀가 범인이라는 것은 매우 충격적이다. (shocking, a criminal)

unit 27 명사절을 이끄는 접속사

4 **간접의문문** : 의문사가 들어가는 명사절을 포함한 문장을 간접의문문이라고 한다.

간접의문문을 만드는데 'think, believe, guess, suppose, say, imagine'이 메인 동사일 경우
의문사가 문장 맨 앞으로 나온다.

- Do you know which kind of sushi he likes?
  너는 어떤 종류의 스시를 그가 좋아하는지 아니?

- Do you think what this is? (x)
- What do you think this is? (o)
  이게 뭐라고 생각하니?

EXERCISE

다음 두 문장을 합쳐서 하나의 간접의문으로 만드세요.

1. Do you know? + Why was she angry?

→

2. I don't know. + When does the school begin?

→

3. I am not sure. + Where is the restroom?

→

4. I don't remember. + What was her e-mail address?

→

5. I wonder. + What time is it now?

→

---- **Exercise 1-1** ---

다음 두 문장을 합쳐서 하나의 간접의문으로 만드세요.

1. I want to know. + Will she come back? (whether)

→

2. Please tell me. + Which car do you like better?

→

3. Do you know? + How old is she?

→

4. She asked me. + How much is the bag?

→

5. I wonder. + Will it rain tonight? (whether)

→

unit 28 형용사절을 이끄는 접속사 (관계대명사)

: 관계대명사는 형용사처럼 명사를 꾸며주는데 항상 뒤에서 앞으로 꾸며준다.

 관계대명사의 종류

	관계대명사	관계대명사 뒤에
주격	who, which, that	주어가 빠진 문장이 옴
소유격	whose, of which	한정사가 빠진 문장이 옴
목적격	who(m), which, that	목적어가 빠진 문장이 옴

★ 한정사: the, a, an, his, their 등
★ 꾸며주는 명사가 사람일 때 who, whose, who(m)을 쓴다.

- Ken is the boy who(that) hates Barbie. (주격)
  켄은 바비를 싫어하는 소년이다.

- Ken is the boy who(m)(that) Barbie hates. (목적격)
  켄은 바비가 싫어하는 소년이다.

- The clock which(that) doesn't tick needs to be repaired. (주격)
  똑딱거리지 않는 저 시계는 수리될 필요가 있다.

- I have a bag which(that) my girl friend made. (목적격)
  나는 내 여자 친구가 만든 가방을 가지고 있다.

 관계대명사의 생략: 목적격 관계대명사는 생략이 가능하다.

- The man (who(m)) I met was George.
- The man who met me was George.

EXERCISE

다음 주어진 문장을 분석하고 해석하세요.

1. I was impressed by a girl who delivered a speech.
→

2. The dog that barks every day is annoying.
→

3. The scientist explained the substance which he found.
→

4. The girl who hid her real intention has bothered me.
→

5. He expects a miracle that will make him pass the exam.
→

---- **Exercise 1-1** --

다음 주어진 문장을 분석하고 해석하세요.

1. I have a watch which I found on the street.
→

2. They got the snake which bit him.
→

3. He relies on a woman who gave him lots of money.
→

4. We are looking for a vet who can cure my dog.
→

5. Anyone who likes to run can join this club.
→

---- **Exercise 2** --

다음 괄호 안에 that을 제외한 적절한 관계대명사를 써 넣으세요.

1. That is the girl (   ) likes to play golf.

2. He is my dad (   ) is working in the garden.

3. I know a man (   ) name is John.

4. The pen (   ) is on the desk is mine.

5. Look at the house (   ) door is blue.

6. The cat (   ) I like most is under the chair.

7. I met an actor (   ) I really wanted to meet.

8. This is the problem (   ) we are worried about.

9. The women (   ) wore high heels were rich.

10. He has an idea (   ) I don't agree with.

---- **Exercise 2-1** --

다음 괄호 안에 that을 제외한 적절한 관계대명사를 써 넣으세요.

1. She is the lady (   ) I met yesterday.

2. He has a son (   ) became an athlete.

3. I will meet a woman (   ) car is convertible KIA.

4. He bought the book (   ) was not in the library.

5. I bought a book (   ) cover is black.

6. Is it the movie (   ) you wanted to see?

7. This is the letter (   ) James wrote.

8. I bought the car (   ) I really wanted to have.

9. The pen (   ) John is using is mine.

10. The house (   ) roof is red is theirs.

unit 29 부사절을 이끄는 접속사

 시간의 부사절(1): when, while, until

종류	when	while	until
뜻	~할 때	~하는 동안	~할 때까지

- When I sent her the first signal, I was excited.
  내가 그녀에게 첫 신호를 보냈을 때, 나는 흥분했다.
- While I was traveling to Venus, I was nervous.
  내가 금성을 여행하는 동안, 나는 긴장되었다.
- Until he got angry, I kept teasing him.
  그가 화날 때까지, 나는 계속해서 그를 놀렸다.

 시간의 부사절(2): before, after

종류	before	after
뜻	~전에	~후에

- He was shy before he met her.
  그는 그녀를 만나기 전엔 수줍음이 많았다.
- He became talkative after he met her.
  그는 그녀를 만난 후엔 수다쟁이가 됐다.

★ before과 after은 전치사로도 쓰인다. 따라서,

- He was shy before meeting her. (o)
- He became talkative after meeting her. (o)

 조건의 부사절: if, unless

종류	if	unless (= if ~ not)
뜻	만약 ~한다면	~하지 않는다면

- If we (will) take a taxi, we will get there faster.

  만약 우리가 택시를 탄다면, 우리는 거기에 더 빨리 도착할거야.

- Unless I go to Japan, I will stay with you.

  = If I don't go to Japan, I will stay with you.

  만약 내가 일본에 가지 않는다면, 너와 함께 있을게.

★ 시간과 조건의 부사절에서는 현재시제가 미래시제를 대신한다.

- When I (will) arrive at the restaurant, I will text you. (시간의 부사절)

  내가 식당에 도착하면, 너에게 문자해줄게.

- If I (will) go to Japan, I will buy you a kimono. (조건의 부사절)

  만약 내가 일본에 가면, 나는 네게 기모노를 사줄게.

- If we (will) take a taxi, we will get there faster. (조건의 부사절)

  만약 우리가 택시를 탄다면, 우리는 거기에 더 빨리 도착할거야.

unit 29 부사절을 이끄는 접속사

4 이유의 부사절: because, as, since: 왜냐하면, ~이기 때문에

- I went to the library because I had an appointment.

  나는 약속이 있기 때문에 도서관에 갔다.

- As I'm a big fan of the singer, I listen to his music all the time.

  나는 그 가수의 열혈 팬이어서, 나는 항상 그의 음악을 듣는다.

- Since I don't like him, I don't want to meet him.

  나는 그를 좋아하지 않기 때문에, 나는 그를 만나기를 원하지 않는다.

★ since는 '~이래로'라는 뜻으로 시간의 부사절로도 쓰이니 헷갈리지 않도록 주의한다.

시간의 부사절을 이끌 때는 보통 주절을 현재완료시제로 쓴다.

- Since I didn't like him, I haven't met him.

  그를 좋아하지 않은 이후로, 나는 그를 만나지 않는다.

5 양보의 부사절: although, even though, though

종류	although, even though, though
뜻	비록 ~라 할지라도

- Although he is rich, he is not generous.

  비록 그가 부유할지라도, 그는 관대하지 않다.

- Though she is pretty, she is rude.

  비록 그녀가 예쁠지라도, 그녀는 무례하다.

- Even though I hate him, we help each other.

  비록 내가 그를 싫어할 지라도, 우리는 서로를 돕는다.

결과의 부사절: so~ that (너무 ~해서 그 결과 ~ 하다)

- He is so kind that everybody loves him a lot.

  그는 너무 친절해서 그 결과 모두가 그를 많이 좋아한다.

- She is so smart that she can solve the complicated math problem.

  그녀는 너무 똑똑해서 그 결과 그 복잡한 수학문제를 풀 수 있다.

- Salt grains are so small that it is very difficult to count every single grain.

  소금 알갱이들은 너무 작아서 그 결과 모든 알갱이를 세는 것은 매우 어렵다.

★ 다양하게 사용되는 접속사 as

a. ~하면서, ~하고 있을 때 (≒ when, while)

- I ate lunch as I watched TV.

  나는 TV를 보면서 점심을 먹었다.

b. ~함에 따라

- She got mature as time went by.

  시간이 지남에 따라 그녀는 성숙해졌다.

c. ~이므로 (≒ because)

- She likes to hang out with friends as she is outgoing.

  그녀는 외향적이므로 친구들과 어울리는 것을 좋아한다.

---- **Exercise 1** --

다음 괄호 안에서 적절한 표현을 고르세요.

1. (When /If) you take a bus, you will be late for the meeting.

2. She was tall (when /if) she was a high school student.

3. (While /If) I was studying with my tutor, my sister was reading a book.

4. She left home (when /if) the sun rose.

5. (Although /When) she saw him, he was smiling at her.

6. (When /Although) I'm an experienced athlete, I'm nervous.

7. (Although /While) I can't live a long life, I will never forget you.

8. (Until /Because) my father buys me the toy, I won't move a step.

9. The game is so easy (when /that) most of people can enjoy it.

10. I was reading a book (when /while) a dog started to bark.

---- **Exercise 1-1** --

다음 빈칸에 적절한 부사절을 이끄는 접속사를 쓰세요.

1. We will leave (when / while) he comes.

2. (Although /Because) they are poor, they seem happy together.

3. He is so strong (when /that) he can lift a car.

4. (Unless / If) you study more, you won't be able to get A.

5. (While /Before) I went to sleep, I had to brush my teeth.

6. (Because /When) I was taking a shower, I noticed someone come in my house.

7. (When /While) I arrived at school, it started to rain.

8. She is so smart (that /when) she can memorize many words at once.

9. I met him (although /because) he had something to give me.

10. (If /Unless) I am late, I can see the superstar.

EXERCISE

---- **Exercise 2** ---

다음 문장을 주어진 단어를 활용하여 영작하세요.

1. 그는 너무 뚱뚱해서 빨리 달리지 못한다. (so fat)

→

2. 만약 날씨가 허락한다면, 우리는 소풍을 갈 것이다. (permit, go on a picnic)

→

3. 그녀는 비록 어리지만, 그녀의 의견을 잘 표현한다. (express one's opinion)

→

4. Tom은 해야 할 일이 너무 많아서 점심을 먹지 않았다. (things)

→

5. 비록 그는 충분히 나이가 들었지만 여전히 만화책 읽는 것을 좋아한다. (still, comic books)

→

EXERCISE

다음 문장을 주어진 단어를 활용하여 영작하세요.

1. 그 문제는 너무 어려워서 아무도 풀지 못한다. (the problem, solve)

→

2. 서두르지 않으면 우리는 그 버스를 놓칠 거다. (hurry, miss)

→

3. 만약 네가 그를 만난다면, 그는 그의 죄를 고백할 것이다. (confess, guilt)

→

4. 그는 매우 키가 커서 농구 선수가 될 수 있다. (a basketball player)

→

5. 그는 매우 많은 돈을 가지고 있어서 그 결과 그는 그 집을 살 수 있다. (much)

→

6. 만약 네가 지금 낮잠을 자지 않으면, 오늘밤에 많이 피곤할 것이다. (take a nap)

→

단원별 문제

Chapter 8 종속접속사

[1-3] 다음 괄호 안에서 알맞은 것을 고르세요.

1 I left school earlier (when / because) I felt sick.

2 Dad cleaned the living room (if / while) mom was cooking dinner.

3 Jin has been interested in musicals (before / since) she joined the club.

4 다음 빈칸에 공통으로 들어갈 말로 알맞은 것은?

- Jin saves money_____he wants to buy a car.
- Sojin has played football_____ she was 5 years old.

① by
② still
③ since
④ for
⑤ until

5 다음 중 밑줄 친 Since의 의미가 나머지와 <u>다른</u> 하나는?

① <u>Since</u> you have a problem, you can't go there.
② She has been stayed here <u>since</u> 2015.
③ I have listened to K-pop music <u>since</u> I was 7 years old.
④ I have read lots of books <u>since</u> I was a 10 years old.
⑤ <u>Since</u> I came here in 2015, I have never read books.

6 다음 빈칸에 들어갈 말로 가장 적절한 것은?

_____Jina is a student, she has to study hard.

① After
② When
③ Before
④ Because
⑤ Until

7 다음 밑줄 친 when의 쓰임이 <보기>와 같은 것은?

<u>When</u> my brother came home, I was talking on the phone.

① <u>When</u> is Jimin's birthday?
② I don't know <u>when</u> to go.
③ <u>When</u> do you think he is coming?
④ <u>When</u> is Jin going to move to Seoul?
⑤ I used to watch movies <u>when</u> I was lonely.

8 다음 중 밑줄 친 부분의 쓰임이 어법상 <u>틀린</u> 것은?

① Make hay <u>while</u> the sun shines.
② Be careful <u>when</u> you walk with the dog.
③ It has been two years <u>since</u> we moved here.
④ She is popular <u>after</u> she is kind.
⑤ <u>After</u> we had pizza, we went shopping.

9 다음 중 어법상 틀린 문장은?

① She woke up when someone knocked the door.
② When you feel sad, cry loudly.
③ I'll take a rest if I have a cold.
④ When my father comes here, I will leave.
⑤ She felt surprised when the accident happens.

[10-11] 다음 빈칸에 들어갈 말로 알맞은 것을 고르세요.

10

Poly makes friends easily_____she is outgoing.

① if
② that
③ while
④ because
⑤ however

11

_____he is generous with money, he doesn't waste his money.

① Although
② When
③ While
④ Until
⑤ By

12 다음 빈칸에 들어갈 말로 가장 적절한 것은?

_____he came back from class, he was surprised at the party.

① While
② Since
③ Because
④ When
⑤ Before

[13-14] 다음 빈칸에 공통으로 들어갈 말로 알맞은 것을 고르세요.

13

• _____I like the girl, I can't look her in the eye.
• I have attended the concert_____2015.

① (B)because
② (S)since
③ (W)when
④ (A)as
⑤ (B)by

14

They asked me_____I was born.

① for
② since
③ when
④ as
⑤ by

[15-16] 다음 빈칸에 들어갈 말로 알맞은 것을 고르세요.

15

_____Somi is very young, she can understand this article.

① If
② Because
③ When
④ Although
⑤ So

16

I'll join the cooking club if you_____ me how to cook.

① shows
② show
③ will show
④ to show
⑤ showing

17 다음 밑줄 친 부분 중 어법상 틀린 것은?

I ①will ②go ③rock climbing ④if it ⑤won't rain tomorrow.

18 다음 빈칸에 들어갈 말이 순서대로 짝지어진 것은?

If you_____the bathroom, I_____the room.

① clean-did
② cleaned-will do
③ cleaned-to do
④ will clean-did
⑤ clean- will do

19 다음 우리말에 맞도록 괄호 안의 단어들을 바르게 배열하세요.

• 아버지가 드시기 시작할 때까지 아무것도 먹지 마라.

→ _____

_____.

(eating / your father / don't eat / until / anything / starts)

20 다음 빈칸에 들어갈 말로 알맞은 것을 모두 고르면?

The children became disappointed_____ they were not chosen to meet the hero.

① while
② since
③ when
④ though
⑤ because

Chapter 8 종속접속사

21 다음 글의 밑줄 친 부분 중 어법상 틀린 것은?

You should ①stop drinking too much alcohol ②and eat more vegetables. ③If you ④will give it a try, you ⑤will be healthier and better.

22 다음 중 밑줄 친 부분과 바꿔 쓸 수 있는 것은?

As I'm still in class, they have to wait for me outside.

① For
② Unless
③ When
④ Though
⑤ Because

23 다음 빈칸에 들어갈 말로 알맞은 것은?

_____because the rewards are huge.

① I ignored the answer
② You'd better not give up
③ I tried to give up
④ I used to answer the question
⑤ The boy caused the trouble

24 다음 우리말을 영어로 바르게 옮긴 것은?

네가 최선을 다한다고 해도 너는 그것을 제 시간에 제출을 못할 것이다.

① When you try your best, you won't be able to hand it in on time.
② Even you do your best, you won't be able to hand it in on time.
③ If you try your best, you won't be able to hand it in on time.
④ Even if you do your best, you won't be able to hand it in on time.
⑤ Unless you do your best, you will be able to hand it in on time.

25 다음 우리말에 맞도록 빈칸에 알맞은 말을 쓰세요.

• 내일 비가 오면 그들은 소풍을 가지 않을 것이다.

→ If _____ _____ tomorrow, they won't go on a picnic.

9 대명사
Chapter

Gorilla Grammar

unit 30 인칭대명사

인칭	수	격	주격 (주어자리)	소유격 (명사수식)	목적격 (목적어자리)	소유대명사	재귀대명사
1인칭	단수		I	my	me	mine	myself
	복수		we	our	us	ours	ourselves
2인칭	단수		you	your	you	yours	yourself
	복수		you	your	you	yours	yourselves
3인칭	단수	남성	he	his	him	his	himself
		여성	she	her	her	hers	herself
		중성	it	its	it		itself
	복수		they	their	them	theirs	themselves

★ 용어설명
- 1인칭: '나(본인)'를 말한다.
- 2인칭: '너(상대방)'를 말한다.
- 3인칭: '나'와 '너'를 제외한 모든 것을 말한다.
- 단수: 한 개
- 복수: 둘 이상

■ 소유대명사의 사용

소유대명사 = 소유격 + 명사

해석은 '~의 것'으로 하며, 명사이므로 주어, 목적어, 보어자리에 들어갈 수 있다.

특히 he는 소유격과 소유대명사의 형태가 모두 'his'이므로 사용에 주의한다.

종류	뜻
mine	나의 것
ours	우리들 것
yours	당신 것, 당신들 것
his	그의 것
hers	그녀의 것
theirs	그들의 것

unit 30 인칭대명사

• I want my key. → mine

나는 나의 열쇠를 원한다. (나는 나의 것을 원한다.)

• They want their keys. → theirs

그들은 그들의 열쇠를 원한다. (그들은 그들의 것을 원한다.)

■ 재귀대명사 관용표현

by oneself	나 혼자, 나 홀로(=alone)
for oneself	혼자 힘으로
enjoy oneself	즐기다
help yourself	마음껏 먹다
of oneself	저절로
between ourselves	우리끼리 얘기지만

■ 재귀대명사의 사용

a. 재귀 용법: 주어와 목적어가 동일할 때 목적어자리에 재귀대명사를 쓴다.

• She consoled herself by shopping. (She = herself)

그녀는 쇼핑함으로써 그녀 자신을 위로했다.

• He always thinks of himself. (He = himself)

그는 항상 자기 자신만을 생각한다.

b. 강조 용법: 문장 구성요소가 아니라 부사로 쓰여 강조, 수식 한다.

따라서 문장에서 제거되어도 대개 문장이 어색하진 않다.

• She herself felt blue.

그녀는 그녀 스스로 우울함을 느꼈다.

• We built the tower ourselves.

우리는 우리 자신이 그 빌딩을 세웠다.

EXERCISE

---- **Exercise 1** --

다음 인칭대명사표의 빈칸을 채우세요.

인칭	격 수		주격 (주어자리)	소유격 (명사수식)	목적격 (목적어자리)	소유대명사	재귀대명사
1인칭	단수		I				
	복수		we				
2인칭	단수		you				
	복수		you				
3인칭	단수	남성	he				
		여성	she				
		중성	it				
	복수		they				

---- **Exercise 1-1** --

다음 인칭대명사표의 빈칸을 채우세요.

인칭	격 수		주격 (주어자리)	소유격 (명사수식)	목적격 (목적어자리)	소유대명사	재귀대명사
1인칭	단수		I				
	복수		we				
2인칭	단수		you				
	복수		you				
3인칭	단수	남성	he				
		여성	she				
		중성	it				
	복수		they				

---- **Exercise 2** --

다음 밑줄 친 부분을 한 단어로 쓰세요.

1. This car is <u>my car</u>. → _____

2. This car is <u>her car</u>. → _____

3. This car is <u>their car</u>. → _____

4. This car is <u>his car</u>. → _____

5. This car is <u>your car</u>. → _____

6. This car is <u>our car</u>. → _____

---- **Exercise 2-1** --

다음 밑줄 친 부분을 한 단어로 쓰세요.

1. This cat is <u>your cat</u>. → _____

2. This cat is <u>their cat</u>. → _____

3. This cat is <u>my cat</u>. → _____

4. This cat is <u>his cat</u>. → _____

5. This cat is <u>our cat</u>. → _____

6. This cat is <u>her cat</u>. → _____

EXERCISE

---- **Exercise 3** --

다음 중 옳은 형태를 고르세요.

1. This bag is (I / my / me / mine).

2. (You / Your / Yours) can do it.

3. Brad Pitt is (he / his / him / himself) favorite actor.

4. He solved the math problem by (his / him / himself).

5. My shoes are larger than (yourself / yours / themselves).

6. Help (you / your / yourself) to some more salad.

7. I went to Japan by (him /myself /yours).

---- **Exercise 3-1** --

다음 중 옳은 형태를 고르세요.

1. Tom forced (me / myself / his) to buy his.

2. She asked (them / his / your) to stay with her.

3. We enjoyed (us / our / ourselves) at this class.

4. This watch is not yours. It's (his / himself / him).

5. I can't make (me / my / mine / myself) understand French.

6. Jane can wash her face by (her / herself / himself) now.

7. I made (your / his / him) a cake.

8. He enjoys (him / his / himself) very much.

| Junior Gorilla Grammar   Level 2

---- **Exercise 4** ---

우리말에 맞게 다음 주어진 문장의 빈칸을 채우세요.

1. 어느 가방이 너의 것이니?
→ Which bag is_____?

2. 나의 시계는 너의 것보다 크다.
→ _____watch is bigger than yours.

3. 너 혼자 그 탁자를 옮길 수 있니?
→ Can you move the table by_____?

4. 그들은 그들의 힘으로 그것을 해야만 한다.
→_____have to do that for_____.

5. 나는 거울 속에 있는 나 자신을 보았다.
→ I saw_____in the mirror.

6. 휴대폰은 스스로 생각할 수 없다.
→ A cell phone can't think for_____.

7. 그들의 집은 매우 크다.
→_____house is very big.

8. 나에게 소금을 건네주세요.
› Pass_____the salt, please.

9. 그들은 오직 그들 자신들만 생각한다.
→ They only think about_____.

EXERCISE

---- **Exercise 4-1** ---

우리말에 맞게 다음 주어진 문장의 빈칸을 채우세요.

1. 이 펜은 나의 것이다.
→ This pen is_____.

2. 하늘은 스스로 돕는 자를 돕는다.
→ Heaven helps those who help _____.

3. 책상 위에 있는 책들은 그의 것이다.
→ The books on the desk are _____.

4. 너와 나는 동갑이다.
→ _____and I are of the same age.

5. 그녀는 자살하였다.
→ She killed _____.

6. 그 창문은 저절로 열렸다.
→ The window opened by _____.

7. 우리의 친구는 공부하는 것을 좋아한다.
→ _____friend likes to study.

8. 나의 것이 그의 것보다 훨씬 작다.
→ _____is much smaller than _____.

9. (음식을) 많이 드세요.
→ Help _____.

unit 31 비인칭 it

: 막연한 날씨, 계절, 날짜, 명암, 시간, 거리, 막연한 상황 등을 나타낼 때 주어자리를 비워두지
않기 위해 사용한다.

- It is raining now. (날씨)
  지금 비가 내리고 있다.

- It is summer now. (계절)
  이제 여름이다.

- It is bright in the living room. (명암)
  거실은 밝다.

- It is three o'clock. (시간)
  세시다.

- It's about 10 kilometers. (거리)
  대략 10킬로미터이다.

- It's August 21st today. (날짜)
  오늘은 8월 21일이다.

EXERCISE

---- **Exercise 1** ---

다음 문장을 it을 활용하여 영작하세요.

1. 지금 비가 오고 있다.

→

2. 서울에서 대전까지 얼마나 멉니까? (from Seoul to Daejun)

→

3. 지금 몇 시입니까?

→

4. 오늘 화창하다. (sunny)

→

---- **Exercise 1-1** ---

다음 문장을 it을 활용하여 영작하세요.

1. 이제 여름이다.

→

2. 지금은 오후 8시 30분입니다.

→

3. 오늘은 날씨가 춥다. (cold)

→

4. 여기서 너의 집까지 얼마나 멉니까?

→

unit 32 부정대명사 1

: 부정대명사는 불특정한 사물이나 사람을 막연하게 지칭하는 대명사이다. 일부 부정대명사는
명사적 역할 뿐 아니라 형용사의 역할도 한다. 또한 부정대명사를 공부할 때 수일치를 특히 조심해야한다.

 ## some /any

	some	any
뜻	약간(의), 몇몇(의)	약간, 어떤, 얼마간(의)
주 사용	긍정문, 권유를 나타내는 의문문	부정문, 의문문, 조건문
품사	대명사, 형용사	

- I ate some of your cookies. (대명사)

  나는 너의 쿠키들 중 약간을 먹었다.

- She didn't eat any of your cookies. (대명사)

  그녀는 너의 쿠키들 중 약간도 먹지 않았다.

- Can I eat any of your cookies? (대명사)

  내가 너의 쿠키들을 약간 먹을 수 있을까?

- I want some milk. (형용사)

  나는 약간의 우유를 원한다.

- I don't want any milk. (형용사)

  나는 약간의 우유도 원하지 않는다.

- Would you like some coffee? (형용사)

  커피 좀 마실래?

EXERCISE

---- **Exercise 1** --

다음 문장에서 some과 any 중 더 적절한 것을 고르세요.

1. Do you want (something / anything) to drink?

2. I heard (some / any) strange sound from the other room.

3. I don't want (some / any) chocolate.

4. I need (some / any) sleep.

5. He doesn't need (some / any) of her help.

6. (Some / Any) people are riding their horses in the yard.

---- **Exercise 1-1** --

다음 문장에서 some과 any 중 더 적절한 것을 고르세요.

1. Why don't you have (some / any) coffee?

2. We don't need (some / any) help from you.

3. You can call me (some / any) time you want.

4. There are (some / any) vacancies in the class.

5. I need to put (some / any) money into my account.

6. I didn't mean for (some / any) of this to happen.

---- **Exercise 2** --

다음 주어진 빈칸에 some과 any 중 더 적절한 것을 적으세요.

1. I have_____books to read.

2. Do you have_____books to read?

3._____of them are from China.

4. I don't see_____of my classmates.

5. Do you have_____good news for me?

6. There aren't_____pens in the drawer.

---- **Exercise 2-1** --

다음 주어진 빈칸에 some과 any 중 더 적절한 것을 적으세요.

1. I bought_____bread at the bakery yesterday.

2. We don't have_____salt.

3._____people go to church every Sunday.

4. If you have_____problem, tell me.

5. I made_____mistakes on the exam.

6. I didn't make_____mistakes on the exam.

2 all /both

	all	both
뜻	모든 사람, 모든 것, 모든	양쪽(의), 둘 다
품사	전치한정사, 대명사, 형용사	
수일치	가산 명사와: 복수 취급	복수취급
	불가산 명사와: 단수 취급	
	형용사 역할일 때: 뒤에 오는 명사에 수일치	

★ 전치 한정사란?

　한정사(the, a, an, his 등) 앞에 놓이는 단어

- All the neighbors often <u>throw</u> a party. (전치 한정사)
  모든 이웃들은 종종 파티를 연다.
- All neighbors often <u>throw</u> a party. (형용사)
  모든 이웃들은 종종 파티를 연다.
- All of the neighbors often <u>throw</u> a party. (대명사)
  이웃들 모두는 종종 파티를 연다.
- All <u>are</u> happy. (대명사)
  모두가 행복하다.
- All <u>is</u> well. (대명사)
  모든 것이 좋다.

★ all은 집합명사이기도 해서 하나의 집합을 의미할 땐 단수로, 집합을 이루는 구성원들에 집중할 땐 복수 취급한다.

- Both my sisters <u>are</u> having fun. (전치 한정사)
  나의 여자형제들 둘 다 즐거워한다.
- Both <u>are</u> having fun. (대명사)
  둘 다 즐거워한다.
- Both of us <u>are</u> having fun. (대명사)
  우리 둘 다 즐거워한다.

---- **Exercise 1** --

다음 문장 속 all과 both의 용법으로 옳은 것을 고르고 해석하세요.

1. I believe that all humans are equal. (전치한정사/형용사/대명사)

→

2. All the plants need light and water. (전치한정사/형용사/대명사)

→

3. Both of the brothers are very smart. (전치한정사/형용사/대명사)

→

4. Both students didn't do the homework. (전치한정사/형용사/대명사)

→

5. All are not happy. (전치한정사/형용사/대명사)

→

---- **Exercise 1-1** ---

다음 문장 속 all과 both의 용법으로 옳은 것을 고르고 해석하세요.

1. Both of us did our best. (전치한정사/형용사/대명사)

→

2. All the students have to turn in the report. (전치한정사/형용사/대명사)

→

3. All dogs are lovely. (전치한정사/형용사/대명사)

→

4. They looked so different, but both were nice. (전치한정사/형용사/대명사)

→

5. Both the teachers are too strict with their students. (전치한정사/형용사/대명사)

→

---- **Exercise 2** ---

all과 both를 활용하여 다음 빈칸을 채우세요.

1. 그 방 안에 있는 모든 좌석들은 비어있다. (seat)

→ _____ _____ _____ in the room are empty.

2. 그녀는 아름답고 지적이다.

→ She is _____ beautiful and intelligent.

3. 둘 다 물을 마시고 있다.

→ _____ are drinking water.

4. 우리 둘 다 행복하다.

→ _____ _____ _____ are happy.

5. 나뭇잎 모두가 떨어졌다.

→ _____ _____ _____ fell.

---- **Exercise 2-1** ---

all과 both를 활용하여 다음 빈칸을 채우세요.

1. 그의 모든 돈들이 이제 쓸모없다.

→ _____ _____ _____ is useless now.

2. 너와 나 둘 다 맞다.

→ _____ you and I are right.

3. John은 영어와 불어 둘 모두 잘한다.

→ Jane is good at _____ English and French.

4. 모든 소년들이 모두 죄책감을 느꼈다.

→ _____ _____ _____ felt guilty.

5. 나는 너희 둘 모두에게 매우 감사하다.

→ I thank _____ of _____ .

unit 32 부정대명사 1

 each / every

	each	every
뜻	각각(의)	모든
품사	대명사, 형용사, 부사	형용사
수일치	단수 취급	

- Each of the soldiers <u>stands</u> straight. (대명사)

  군인들 각각은 똑바로 서있다.

- Each <u>stands</u> straight. (대명사)

  각각은 똑바로 서있다.

- Each soldier <u>stands</u> straight. (형용사)

  각각의 군인은 똑바로 서있다.

- I gave them two bananas each. (부사)

  나는 그들에게 두 개의 바나나를 각각 주었다.

- Every pond <u>has</u> lots of fish. (형용사)

  모든 연못은 많은 물고기를 가지고 있다.

- Every has lots of fish. (x)

- -

★ every 단수 취급 예외

> every + 숫자 + 복수명사: ~마다

- The market takes place <u>every</u> five <u>days.</u>

  그 시장은 5일 마다 열린다.

---- **Exercise 1** --

다음 문장의 밑줄 친 부분을 바르게 고쳐 쓰세요.

1. Every <u>ships</u> in the sea began to speed up.

2. Each of the <u>student</u> should have his own book.

3. The World Cup is held <u>each</u> 4 years.

4. Each of us <u>have</u> our own dreams.

5. After every <u>classes</u>, I review what I learned.

6. Everybody <u>hate</u> waking up early in the morning.

7. The shuttle bus comes around every 30 <u>minute</u>.

8. I was touched by every <u>words</u> that he said.

EXERCISE

---- **Exercise 1-1** --

빈칸에 적절한 단어를 보기에서 골라 채워 넣으세요. (둘 다 가능할 수 있음)

보 기
each, every

1. _____ of the students studies hard.

2. _____ class in school is doing fine.

3. _____ studied hard and received good grades by the test.

4. The teacher gave _____ of the students a candy.

5. The train leaves _____ hour.

6. _____ reporter is honest.

7. _____ student knows how to behave.

8. _____ of the students get the guide from school.

9. _____ Sunday, the shop has a discount on fish.

---- **Exercise 2** --

다음 문장의 빈칸을 채우세요.

1. 모든 사람은 투표할 권리를 가진다. (person, have)
→ _____ _____ _____right to vote.

2. 우리들은 각자 10달러씩 받았다.
→ We received 10 dollars _____.

3. 모든 인간은 완벽하지 않다. (human being)
→ _____ _____ _____ not perfect.

4. 각자 다른 스타일을 가진다.
→ _____ _____ different style.

5. 모든 학생들은 열심히 공부한다.
→ _____ _____ _____ hard.

---- **Exercise 2-1** --

다음 문장의 빈칸을 채우세요.

1. 각각의 문제는 20점을 준다. (question, give)
→ _____ _____ _____ 20 point.

2. 나는 우리 학교의 모든 학생을 안다.
→ I know _____ _____at my school.

3. 나는 모든 순간을 즐긴다. (minute)
→ I enjoy _____ _____.

4. 나는 신문의 모든 기사를 다 읽었다. (article)
→ I read _____ _____ on the newspaper.

5. 우리는 각각 용돈을 40달러씩 받는다.
→ _____ of _____ receives 40 dollars as pocket money.

it과 one : it은 바로 그것을 가리킴, one은 그것과 같은 종류의 것을 가리킴.

I lost my notebook.

- about one) I need a notebook, so I have to buy **one**.

  나는 노트가 필요해(잃어버린 그 노트가 아니더라도) 그래서 나는 하나 사야겠어.

- about it) There are many important things in it. I have to find it.

  그것(내가 잃어버린 그 노트)안에는 중요한 것이 많아. 나는 그것을 찾아야만해.

a. it과 one의 복수형

it	they /them
one	ones

These shoes are too small for me.

- about ones)   Could you bring me bigger ones?

  조금 더 큰 **것들**(같은 종류)로 갖다 주실래요?

- about they /them) But it's ok. They are for my brother. I'll buy them.

  하지만 괜찮아. 그것들(바로 그것)은 내 남자 형제를 위한 거야. 그것들을 살게요.

---- **Exercise 1** --

빈칸에 적절한 단어를 보기에서 골라 채워 넣으세요.

보 기
one, it, ones, them

1. I would like to buy a skirt. Can you recommend_____?

2. I need your notebook. Can I use_____?

3. She requires a dictionary for her study. I want to buy_____for her.

4. I lost all my pens. I need a red pen and two blue_____for writing.

5. I put all your books in the box, so you can find_____in_____ .

6. I want to buy_____among these shoes. But I can't decide. They are all pretty.

7. I heard that you have a lot of clothes. Can I borrow_____ of them?

8. Do you know where Mike and Susan are? I can't find_____.

9. I can't find my sister's favorite bag. I think I lost_____.

10. Although the cheese smells too strong, I want to taste_____.

EXERCISE

---- **Exercise 1-1** --

빈칸에 적절한 단어를 보기에서 골라 채워 넣으세요.

보 기
one, it, ones, them

1. I need a yellow umbrella and three white_____.

2. I lost my ticket. I have to buy_____right now.

3. I had lost my ticket, but I found_____in the toilet.

4. I had lost my tickets, but I found _____in the toilet.

5. These gloves are so pretty. Can I try_____ ?

6. These pants look too small for me. Are there bigger_____?

7. I need a new cell-phone. Dad, could you buy me_____?

8. You learned 10 words today. Please memorize_____until next time.

9. This skirt is too small for me. I need a bigger _____ .

10. The movie seems interesting. I want to see_____ .

240 | Junior Gorilla Grammar   Level 2

---- **Exercise 1-2** --

빈칸에 적절한 단어를 보기에서 골라 채워 넣으세요.

보 기
one, it, ones, them

1. These shoes are worn out too much. I need bigger_____.

2. I bought a new MP3. I will lend_____to you.

3. This picture is the oldest_____that I have.

4. This picture is so important to me. I can't give_____to you.

5. All bananas at home decayed, so I threw_____away.

6. All clothes in the closet are worn out. I've got to buy new_____.

7. A: Have you read the books he lent? B: No, I haven't read_____yet.

8. These are some pencils. Can I use black_____?

9. These movies are not interesting. I will download other_____.

10. I downloaded three movies yesterday. Would you see_____with me?

2 **one~, the other...** : (둘 중에서) 하나는~, 나머지 하나는...

- There are <u>two</u> apples. One is for me, the other is for you.

  두 개의 사과가 있다. 하나는 나를 위한 것이고, 나머지 하나는 너를 위한 것이다.

3 **one~, the others...** : (둘 이상에서) 하나는~, 나머지 전부는...

- There are <u>four</u> apples. One is for me, the others are for you.

  네 개의 사과가 있다. 하나는 나를 위한 것이다, 나머지 전부는 너를 위한 것이다.

4 **one~, another..., the other-** : (셋 이상에서) 하나는~, 또 다른 하나는...,
  나머지 하나(마지막 남은 것)는-

- There are <u>four</u> apples. One is for me, another is for him, another is for her,

  and the other is for you.

  네 개의 사과가 있다. 하나는 나를 위한 것이고, 또 다른 하나는 그를 위한 것이고,

  또 다른 하나는 그녀를 위한 것이고, 나머지 하나는 너를 위한 것이다.

5 ① **some~, other(s)...** : 일부는~, 또 다른 일부는...
  ② **some~, the others...** : 일부는~, 나머지 전부는...

- In the world, some like to play soccer and others like to play basketball.
= In the world, some people like to play soccer and other people like to play basketball.

  세상에서, 일부 사람들을 축구하는 것을 좋아하고, 또 다른 일부는 농구하는 것을 좋아한다.

  (그 외에 사람들은 또 다른 것을 좋아하겠지.)

- In the classroom, today, some will stay more after school and the others will go home.

  그 학급에서 오늘 일부는 방과 후에 남을 것이고 나머지 전부는 집에 갈 것이다.

---- **Exercise 1** --

빈칸에 적절한 단어를 보기에서 골라 채워 넣으세요.

1. Some people like summer and_____like winter.

2. There are two books. One is mine and_____is for you.

3. This sandwich is delicious! Can I have_____sandwich?

4. There are 6 computers in the class. Only one computer works properly, and
_____ all broke down.

5. I know three foreigners. One is Japanese,_____is French, and
_____is American.

6. Please try to be kind to_____around you.

7. Only you and I know this secret._____in the class do not know.

8. If you fail this time, you will not get_____chance.

9. There are five rats in the cage. Two of them have orange fur, and_____
have black fur.

10. I need to find two books. One is a history book, and_____is a science book.

EXERCISE

---- **Exercise 1-1** ---

빈칸에 적절한 단어를 보기에서 골라 채워 넣으세요.

보 기
other, others, the other, the others, another

1. I have two brothers. One is Austin and_____is John.

2. He had five pens in the pencil case. One was black and_____were all red.

3. Some people eat meat while_____don't.

4. I have three balls in my room. One is a baseball,_____is a basketball, and_____is a soccer ball.

5. I have two computers in my room. One is a desktop computer, and _____is a laptop computer.

6. After class, only one student was left in the classroom while_____ went home.

7. I wrote a letter to my parents. Then, I wrote_____letter to my best friend.

8. I have two pets at home. One is a dog and_____is a cat.

9. There were many people at the park. Some people were taking a walk while _____were lying in the grass.

10. Two roads diverged in the woods. Some people took the left road while _____took the right.

---- **Exercise 1-2** --

빈칸에 적절한 단어를 보기에서 골라 채워 넣으세요.

보 기
other, others, the other, the others, another

1. I have two pens. _____is black, and_____is blue.

2. There are three people walking on the road. _____is tall,_____is wearing a cap,_____isn't wearing shoes.

3. Only one student out of ten did the homework. _____did nothing.

4. In the meeting, _____people can play the piano, and_____ can do the violin.

5._____ agreed with me, but_____didn't.

6. I met two people yesterday. _____came from France, and_____ came from Italy.

7. I have three elder sisters. _____is 25 years old,_____is 22 years old, and_____is 20 years old.

8. There are 4 cups on the table. _____is full, but _____are empty.

9. I bought a rose for my mother, and_____for my girlfriend.

10. My family has 5 members. Father lives with me, and_____live in a different place.

1 다음 빈칸에 들어갈 말로 바르게 짝지어진 것은?

I've been to two cities. _____was Beijing and_____was Bangkok.

① One - other
② One - others
③ Some - others
④ One - the other
⑤ Some - the others

2 다음 우리말과 일치하도록 빈칸에 알맞은 말을 쓰세요.

• 그 컴퓨터는 지난번에 저절로 켜졌다.
→ The computer started _____last time.

3 다음 빈칸에 공통으로 들어갈 말로 알맞은 것은?

• _____is pink. The other is purple.
• Which_____is better?

① (T)this
② (T)that
③ (O)one
④ (O)ones
⑤ (I)it

4 다음 빈칸에 들어갈 말로 알맞은 것은?

• How's your marriage going these days?
→ It's not that bad. How about_____?

① it
② others
③ yours
④ your
⑤ the one

5 다음 빈칸에 공통으로 들어갈 대명사를 쓰세요.

• The jean is too big for me. Show me
_____ .
• I'm still tired. Please give me _____
energy drink.

6 다음 빈칸에 들어갈 말로 알맞은 것은?

A: Which is her car? Is that_____?
B: No, her car is parked in the garage.

① mine
② yours
③ one
④ hers
⑤ his

7 다음 빈칸에 들어갈 말로 바르게 짝지어진 것은?

> I borrowed four comic books._____is
> Dragon ball and_____are romantic ones.

① One - another
② One - the others
③ Another - the other
④ The other - another
⑤ Another - the others

8 다음 밑줄 친 부분의 우리말 뜻이 **틀린** 것은?

① He scored a goal <u>for himself</u>. (혼자 힘으로)
② He lives in that penthouse <u>by himself</u>. (혼자서)
③ If you want more Coke, <u>help yourself</u>. (마음껏 먹다)
④ <u>Between ourselves</u>, Jack is a nut. (사실대로 말하자면)
⑤ He <u>enjoyed himself</u> at the Latino festival. (즐거운 시간을 보냈다)

9 다음 밑줄 친 It의 쓰임이 나머지 넷과 <u>다른</u> 것은?

① <u>It</u> is already ten thirty.
② <u>It</u> is sunny today.
③ <u>It</u> is winter now.
④ <u>It</u> will get bright soon.
⑤ <u>It</u> is easy to answer his question.

10 다음 빈칸에 들어갈 말로 바르게 짝지어진 것은?

> • Do you have_____problems?
> • I don't like it. Show me_____.

① other - other
② one - another
③ another - other
④ other - another
⑤ another - another

11 다음 빈칸에 공통으로 들어갈 말로 알맞은 것은?

> • I watch TV_____day.
> • The train runs_____10 minutes.

① every
② all
③ each
④ other
⑤ another

12 다음 밑줄 친 <u>one</u>이 가리키는 것을 우리말로 쓰세요.

> Jeffrey was at a toy store. There were many toy swords. He bought <u>one</u>.
>
> →

13 다음 빈칸에 들어갈 말을 적으세요.

A: What does he do?
B: _____, he is out of a job now.
(우리끼리 얘기지만)

[14-16] 다음 주어진 한국말에 맞게 빈칸을 채우세요.

14 그녀에 의해서 사용되는 그 펜은 그의 것이다.

→ The pen used by her is_____.

15 그는 혼자서 여행을 떠났다.

→ He took a trip by_____.

16 우리의 것들이 깡패들에 의해 파괴되었다.

→_____ were ruined by the bullies.

17 다음 빈칸에 들어갈 말로 알맞은 것은?

A: Which one is the wrong answer, this one
   or that one?
B: _____are wrong.

① Both
② Either
③ Every
④ Any
⑤ What

18 다음 빈칸에 들어갈 말로 알맞은 것은?

You need to clean the snow in front of
your house. Kids and seniors can easily
slip on the ice and hurt_____.

① them
② they
③ their
④ theirs
⑤ themselves

19 다음 보기의 밑줄 친 부분과 쓰임이 같은 것은?

It snowed on and off today.

① It is my father's bag.
② It is a kind of holiday.
③ It is easy to play golf.
④ It is my car.
⑤ It is good to help the poor.

20 다음 빈칸에 들어갈 말로 바르게 짝지어진 것은?

• Jessica and Tiffany understand_____
  other.
• _____of my classes end at 11:30 pm.

① every - All
② each - All
③ each - Each

④ all - Every
⑤ each - Every

21 다음 빈칸에 들어갈 말로 알맞은 것은?

> My daughter already has a smart phone, but she wants to buy_____.

① other
② another
③ the other
④ the others
⑤ one another

[22-24] 빈칸에 들어갈 알맞은 것을 고르세요.

22

> I had lost my old camera, but this morning I found_____in my drawer.

① it
② one
③ another
④ other
⑤ the other

23

> I have two brothers, and_____of them enjoy playing games.

① any
② each
③ both
④ every
⑤ some

24

> We really enjoyed_____at the party.

① we
② our
③ us
④ ours
⑤ ourselves

25 빈칸에 공통으로 들어갈 말로 알맞은 것은?

> • _____student in school likes Mrs. Lee.
> • Sally and I go out_____Saturday night.

① (S)some
② (A)any
③ (B)both
④ (E)every
⑤ (A)all

10 비교급
Chapter

- unit 34. 비교
- unit 35. 최상급

Gorilla Grammar

unit 34 비교

: 두 가지 이상의 것을 비교할 때 보통 형용사나 부사의 형태가 바뀐다.

1 비교급과 최상급 만들기

a. 규칙 변화

	형용사 /부사	비교급	최상급
1음절: -er, -est *-e로 끝나는 단어: **-r, -st**	smart	smarter	smartest
	young	younger	youngest
	wise	wiser	wisest
<단모음+단자음> 으로 끝나는 단어: 자음을 한 번 더 쓰고 **-er, -est**	big	bigger	biggest
	sad	sadder	saddest
	hot	hotter	hottest
<자음+y>로 끝나는 단어: -y → **-ier, iest**	pretty	prettier	prettiest
	happy	happier	happiest
3음절 이상이거나 -ish, -ful, -ous, -ing 등 으로 끝나는 단어: 앞에 **more, most**를 붙인다	careful	more careful	most careful
	famous	more famous	most famous
	surprising	more surprising	most surprising

b. 불규칙 변화

형용사 /부사	비교급	의미	최상급	의미
good /well	better	더 좋은	best	최고의
ill /bad	worse	더 나쁜	worst	최악의
many /much	more	더	most	가장, 최대의
little	less	덜	least	가장 적은, 최소의

---- **Exercise 1** --

다음 주어진 단어의 비교급과 최상급을 만드세요.

1. healthy　　→　　_____　　_____

2. cool　　→　　_____　　_____

3. strong　　→　　_____　　_____

4. many/much　　→　　_____　　_____

5. few　　→　　_____　　_____

6. small　　→　　_____　　_____

7. weak　　→　　_____　　_____

8. late　　→　　_____　　_____

9. rough　　→　　_____　　_____

10. helpful　　→　　_____　　_____

---- **Exercise 1-1** --

다음 주어진 단어의 비교급과 최상급을 만드세요.

1. young   → _____   _____

2. hard   → _____   _____

3. cold   → _____   _____

4. stylish   → _____   _____

5. cute   → _____   _____

6. hungry   → _____   _____

7. wise   → _____   _____

8. difficult   → _____   _____

9. interesting   → _____   _____

10. old   → _____   _____

unit 34 비교

2 원급 비교 : 동등한 둘을 비교할 때 쓰며, 형용사나 부사 원형을 그대로 사용해서 원급 비교이다.

★ as 나 than 뒤에는 주어 + 동사 또는 목적격이 온다.

| as + 원급(형용사/부사) + as | ~만큼 ~한(하게) |

- She is as smart as her sister (is).

  그녀는 그녀의 여자형제 만큼 똑똑하다.

- I don't play computer games as often as my brother (does).

  나는 내 남자형제가 하는 것만큼 자주 컴퓨터 게임을 하지 않는다.

3 비교 : 두 가지 이상을 비교할 때 쓴다.

| 형용사나 부사의 비교급 + than | ~보다 ~한(하게) |

- She is smarter than her sister (is).

  그녀는 그녀의 여자형제 보다 더 똑똑하다.

- I don't play computer games more often than my brother (does).

  나는 내 남자형제가 하는 것보다 더 자주 컴퓨터 게임을 하지 않는다.

4 비교급 강조 수식어 : 비교급 앞에 위치시켜 '훨씬'이라고 해석하여 비교급을 강조.

much, even, still, far, a lot 등

- She is much younger than I am.

  그녀는 나보다 훨씬 어리다.

- My bag is even more expensive than hers.

  나의 가방은 그녀의 것보다 훨씬 더 비싸다.

---- **Exercise 1** --

다음 문장을 문법적으로 옳게 고치세요.

1. Tom is tall than Jane.
→

2. The boy is more strong than he was last year.
→

3. This screen is wide than that one.
→

4. This box is more big than the refrigerator.
→

5. Suzy is prettyer than Kelly.
→

---- **Exercise 1-1** --

다음 문장을 문법적으로 옳게 고치세요.

1. Celine is much oldest than her.
→

2. This watch is expensiver than that car.
→

3. She is more beautiful she was three years ago.
→

4. This building is tall than the tower.
→

5. This restroom is more clean than the living room.
→

EXERCISE

다음 문장을 문법적으로 옳게 고치세요.

1. She is as stronger as the athlete.

→

2. They are very more famous than the singers.

→

3. The box is as heavy the cat.

→

4. She is a lot of more intelligent than he is.

→

5. Kim is many hungrier than you think.

→

unit 35 최상급

: 최상급은 보통 한정된 범위를 제안하고 그 제안된 범위에서 최고라는 표현이 되기 때문에 최상급 앞에 한정사 the를 붙인다.

 ## 최상급의 구성

- The + 최상급 + of + (all) 복수명사
- The + 최상급 + (명사) + in 장소
- The + 최상급 + 명사 + (that) ~ever /can
- The + 서수 + 최상급 + in 장소

- Linda is the most beautiful of all the girls.

  Linda는 모든 소녀들 중에서 가장 아름답다.

- She is the most beautiful girl in the world.

  그녀는 세상에서 가장 아름다운 소녀이다.

- Linda is the most beautiful girl (that) I have ever seen.

  Linda는 내가 봐온 가장 아름다운 소녀이다.

- July is the second most beautiful in the world.

  July는 세상에서 두 번째로 아름답다.

- He is one of the most famous artists of the 20th century.

  그는 20세기의 가장 유명한 예술가 중에 하나이다.

- She is one of the youngest professors at the university.

  그녀는 그 대학에서 가장 어린 교수들 중의 하나이다.

2 비교급으로 최상급 표현하기

- 비교급 + than any other + 단수명사
- 비교급 + than all + the + other + 복수명사
- 비교급 + than + anyone else
- No (other) + 단수명사 + 동사 + 비교급 + than 주어

• Nate is taller than any other boy in the class.

Nate는 학급에서 어떤 아이보다 더 키가 크다.

= No boy in the class is taller than Nate.

학급에서 어떤 아이도 Nate보다 크지 않다.

= No boy in the class is as tall as Nate.

학급에서 어떤 아이도 Nate만큼 크지 않다.

= Nate is the tallest boy in the class.

Nate는 학급에서 가장 키가 큰 아이이다.

---- **Exercise 1** --

두 문장이 같은 의미가 되도록 빈칸을 채우시오.

1. No other building in the city is higher than John's building.

 = John's building is (   ) (   ) in the city.

2. Love is the most important thing in my life.

 = Nothing in my life is (   ) important (   ) love.

3. Nothing is as valuable as money.

 = Money is (   ) (   ) valuable of all.

4. She is not as smart as her sister.

 = Her sister is (   ) than she is.

5. The Pacific ocean is the largest ocean on the earth.

 = No ocean on the earth is (   ) (   ) the Pacific ocean.

6. Tokyo is bigger than any other city in Japan.

 = Tokyo is (   ) (   ) city in Japan.

 = (   ) city is (   ) than Tokyo in Japan.

---- **Exercise 1-1** --

두 문장이 같은 의미가 되도록 빈칸을 채우세요.

1. Jane is prettier than any other girl in her class.

= Jane is (　　　　　) (　　　　　　) girl in her class.

2. The blue rose is the most gorgeous flower in my garden.

= (　　　) flower is (　　　) gorgeous (　　　) the blue rose in my garden.

3. Tom speaks English the most fluently in this company.

= No one in this company speaks English (　　　) fluently (　　　) Tom does.

4. Mark Hunt is the strongest fighter in New Zealand.

= No one in New Zealand is (　　　　) (　　　　) Mark Hunt.

5. I have never had such a delicious apple.

= This apple is (　　　　) (　　　　) (　　　　) apple I have ever had.

---- **Exercise 2** --

다음 주어진 문장의 빈칸을 채우세요.

1. 이 초콜릿은 저것보다 달다.

→ This chocolate is_____ _____ that one.

2. 건강은 돈보다 중요하다.

→ Health is_____ _____ _____ money.

3. 그녀는 나보다 훨씬 예쁘다.

→ She is_____ _____ _____ me.

4. 그는 나의 학급에서 가장 키가 크다.

→ He is_____ _____ _____ in my class.

5. 저기서의 경관이 여기서의 경관보다 더 좋다. (spectacular)

→ The scene there is_____ _____ _____ the scene here.

6. 너는 지금보다 더 빨리 수영할 수 있니?

→ Can you swim_____ _____ now?

7. 그녀의 언니는 그녀보다 3살이 많다.

→ Her sister is_____ _____ _____ _____ she is.

EXERCISE

---- **Exercise 2-1** ---

다음 주어진 문장의 빈칸을 채우세요.

1. 돌고래는 바다에서 가장 빠른 동물들 중 하나이다.

→ The dolphin is_____ of _____ _____ animals in the sea.

2. 제주도는 한국에서 가장 큰 섬이다.

→ Jeju island is_____ _____ island in Korea.

3. 사랑이 내 삶에서 가장 중요한 것이다.

→ Love is _____ _____ _____ thing in my life.

4. 이 우유는 저 주스만큼 시원하지 않다.

→ This milk is_____ _____as_____ _____ _____ that juice is.

5. 이 가방은 셋 중에서 가장 비싸다.

→ This bag is _____ _____ _____ of these three bags.

6. 그녀는 세계에서 최고의 가수다.

→ She is _____ _____ _____ in the world.

7. Jane은 그 선생님만큼이나 똑똑하다.

→ Jane is _____ _____ _____ the teacher is.

[1-2] 다음 중 비교급과 최상급의 형태가 틀린 것은?

1
① heavy - heavier - heaviest
② big - biger - bigest
③ fast - faster - fastest
④ slow - slower - slowest
⑤ large - larger - largest

2
① late - later - last
② many - more - most
③ ill - worse - worst
④ good - better - best
⑤ little - latter - last

3 다음 빈칸에 들어갈 말로 알맞은 것은?

> Walking upstairs is not_____walking downstairs.

① easier
② the easiest
③ as easy so
④ as easier as
⑤ as easy as

4 다음 두 문장의 뜻이 일치하도록 빈칸에 알맞은 말을 쓰세요.

> • Minsoo is stronger than Bomi.
> • Bomi is not_____ _____ _____Minsoo.

5 다음 중 어법상 틀린 것은?

① She has more money than you have.
② Ted is the most handsome boy of all.
③ His cell phone is as heavier as mine.
④ She is not as pretty as her sister is.
⑤ August is the hottest month of the year.

6 다음 빈칸에 공통으로 들어갈 말로 알맞지 않은 것은? (2개)

> • A giraffe's neck is_____longer than mine.
> • Korea is_____smaller than China.
> • A car is_____faster than a bike.

① very
② much
③ well
④ far
⑤ even

7 다음 빈칸에 들어갈 말로 알맞은 것은?

> This building is_____any other
> building.

① the most
② other than
③ higher than
④ the highest
⑤ as higher as

8 다음 빈칸에 들어갈 말로 알맞지 <u>않은</u> 것은?

> The exam in history was more _____
> than I expected.

① hard
② helpful
③ interesting
④ difficult
⑤ creative

9 다음 빈칸에 들어갈 말로 알맞은 것은?

> Little Prince is_____ interesting
> book that I have ever read.

① the most
② the more
③ best
④ very
⑤ much

10 다음 밑줄 친 단어의 형태가 바르게 짝지어진 것은?

> • Collin is <u>old</u> of four children.
> • New year's day is one of <u>famous</u> holidays.

① the eldest - more famous
② elder   - more famous
③ the eldest - famous
④ elder   - the most famous
⑤ the eldest - the most famous

11 다음 중 어법상 <u>틀린</u> 것은? (답 2개)

① Jimmy is stronger than I thought.
② She is more beautiful than my sister.
③ Baseball is more popular than soccer in korea.
④ He is more ugly than his brother.
⑤ Time is important than any other thing.

12 다음 빈칸에 들어갈 말로 바르게 짝지어진 것은?

> Gold is_____expensive and beautiful, but
> diamond is_____more expensive and
> beautiful.

① far-still
② very-very
③ even-much
④ very-even
⑤ much-very

[13-14] 다음 글을 읽고, 물음에 답하세요.

Although the bodies of apes are similar to those of humans, their arms are longer and their legs are shorter. Their skulls are (A) thick than humans', but their brains are not as (B)large as humans'. Anyway, (C)is, animal, strongest, the apes, of, the, the gorilla, biggest, and.

13 위 글 (A)와 (B)의 형태가 바르게 짝지어진 것은?

① more thick-large
② more thick-larger
③ thicker-large
④ thicker-larger
⑤ thickest-largest

14 다음 우리말과 일치하도록 (C)의 단어와 어구를 배열하세요.

고릴라는 유인원 중 가장 크고 강한 동물이다.

15 다음 밑줄 친 단어의 형태가 바르게 짝지어진 것은?

• A squirrel is one of cute animals in the world.
• There is a contest for ugly cat in the world.

① cute - ugly
② cuter - uglier
③ the cutest - the ugliest
④ the most cute - ugliest
⑤ the cutest - the most ugly

16 다음 우리말과 일치하도록 할 때 빈칸에 들어갈 말로 알맞은 것은?

• 피카소는 세계에서 가장 위대한 화가 중 한명이다.
→ Picasso is one of the_____ painters in the world.

① well
② better
③ greater
④ greatest
⑤ most

17 다음 중 어법상 틀린 것은?

① Geojedo is one of the most beautiful islands in Korea.
② No island in Korea is as beautiful as Gageodo.
③ No island in Korea is more beautiful than Geojedo.
④ Geojedo is more beautiful than all the other islands in Korea.
⑤ Geojedo is more beautiful than any other islands in Korea.

18 다음 두 문장의 뜻이 일치하도록 빈칸에 알맞은 말을 쓰세요.

• Walking is faster than any other way.
→ Walking is_____. (3단어)

[19-21] 다음 표를 보고, 지시에 따라 문장을 완성하세요.

	Age	Height	Weight
Min	27	161cm	57kg
Jin	33	179cm	77kg
Soo	30	175cm	79kg

19 Soo와 Min의 나이 비교 표현. (old 활용)

→ Soo_____.

20 Jin과 Min의 키 비교 표현. (tall 활용)

→ Jin_____.

21 세 명 중 가장 몸무게가 많이 나가는 사람 표현.
(최상급 비교 사용, heavy)

→ _____.

[22-23] 다음 밑줄 친 부분의 단어와 어구를 배열하여 문장을 완성하세요.

22

• Jin doesn't study hard, but she <u>does, better, I do, than, always</u> on tests.

→She_____
on tests.

23

• Gold is sometimes <u>more, three, than, times, expensive</u> silver.

→ Gold is sometimes _____

_____ silver.

24 다음 우리말과 일치하도록 빈칸에 알맞은 말을 쓰세요.

• Kelly는 학급친구들 중에서 가장 부지런하다.
(diligent)
→ Kelly is_____ _____ _____
of all her classmates.

25 다음 두 문장이 같은 뜻이 되도록 빈칸에 알맞은 단어를 쓰세요.

• Harry and Gabriel are both 175cm tall.

→ Harry is_____ _____ _____
Gabriel.

주니어 고릴라 영문법
Junior Gorilla Grammar

주니어
고릴라
영문법

Junior Gorilla Grammar

level 2

| 정답 및 해설 |

Chapter 1 문장의 구성

Unit 1 단어의 종류

Exercise 1) 다음 제시된 단어들의 종류를 하나만 쓰세요.
1. 명사
2. 동사
3. 형용사
4. 형용사
5. 부사
6. 명사
7. 부사
8. 명사
9. 명사
10. 동사

Exercise 1-1) 다음 제시된 단어들의 종류를 하나만 쓰세요.
1. 형용사
2. 부사
3. 동사
4. 명사 또는 동사
5. 동사
6. 형용사
7. 형용사
8. 형용사
9. 명사
10. 동사

Unit 2 문장의 종류

(1) 문장의 종류
(2) 문장의 구성

Unit 3 1형식과 2형식

(1) 1형식
(2) 2형식

Exercise 1)

다음 문장들이 몇 형식 문장인지 밝히고 해석하세요.
1. (1형식) 새는 난다.
2. (2형식) 그녀는 정직하다.
3. (2형식) 그들은 자유로움을 느꼈다.
4. (2형식) 나는 바쁘다.
5. (2형식) 그들은 취했다.
6. (1형식) 그녀는 천국에 있다.
7. (2형식) 그녀는 천사다.
8. (2형식) Tom은 선생님이 되었다.
9. (2형식) 이 우유는 상했다.
10. (1형식) 나는 일요일에 교회에 갔다.

★전치사 + 명사 = 부사. 부사는 문장필수구성요소가 아님

Exercise 1-1)

다음 문장들이 몇 형식 문장인지 밝히고 해석하세요.
1. (1형식) 오늘 해는 6시에 졌다.
2. (2형식) 그녀는 그들 사이에서 아름답게 보인다.
3. (1형식) 그 남자는 수영장에서 수영을 했다.
4. (2형식) 나의 아들은 의사가 되었다.
5. (1형식) 나는 열심히 노력했어.
6. (1형식) 나는 그것을 신경 쓰지 않아.
7. (1형식) 시간은 날아간다. (시간은 너무 빨리 가.)
8. (2형식) 우리는 부자가 아니다.
9. (2형식) 그 나뭇잎들은 붉고 노랗게 변했다.
10. (2형식) 여름에 날씨가 더워진다.

Exercise 2) 다음 문장을 문법적으로 옳게 고치세요.
1. like 삭제 (이 덮개는 부드러운 느낌이 난다.)
2. like a movie star (그녀는 영화배우처럼 보인다.)
3. like 삭제 (이 샴푸는 좋은 향기가 난다.)
4. greatly → great (그것은 좋은 생각처럼 들린다.)
5. like 삭제 (그 별들은 밝은 것처럼 보인다.)

Exercise 2-1) 다음 문장을 문법적으로 옳게 고치세요.
1. sweetly → sweet (이 사과는 달콤한 맛이 난다.)
2. like 삭제 (이 상품은 부드러운 느낌이 난다.)
3. like 삭제 (이 자동차는 비싸 보인다.)
4. like 삭제 (몇몇의 건강식품은 쓴 맛이 난다.)
5. like 삭제 (그 소년은 행복해 보인다.)

Exercise 3)
다음 주어진 문장을 영작하세요. (예시답안입니다.)
1. John sleeps every day.
2. Time flies like an arrow.
3. She looks like a singer.
4. This pillow feels soft.
5. This bread looks delicious.

Exercise 3-1)
다음 주어진 문장을 영작하세요. (예시답안입니다.)
1. My mom looks young.
2. The sun rises in the east.
3. They always sing in the room.
4. There is a cat under the chair.
5. Leaves turn green in spring.

Unit 4 3형식과 4형식
(1) 3형식
(2) 4형식

Exercise 1)
다음 문장들이 몇 형식 문장인지 밝히고 해석하세요.
1. (4형식) Terry은 나에게 비밀을 하나 말해줬다.
2. (4형식) 나의 남자친구는 나에게 장미꽃 다발을 사줬다.
3. (3형식) 나는 설거지를 했다.
4. (3형식) 우리는 그 진실을 안다.
5. (4형식) 그들은 나에게 돈을 빌려줬다.

2 JUNIOR GORILLA GRAMMAR 2

Exercise 1-1)
다음 문장들이 몇 형식 문장인지 밝히고 해석하세요.
1. (3형식) 그들은 나를 많이 사랑한다.
2. (4형식) 그는 나에게 책을 던졌다.
3. (3형식) 그 용의자는 그의 죄를 인정하지 않았다.
4. (4형식) 그 사회자는 나의 아들에게 은메달을 수여했다.
5. (3형식) 나의 엄마는 그녀의 머리카락을 헤어드라이어로 말렸다.

(3) 4형식을 3형식으로 전환
Exercise 1) 다음 4형식 문장을 3형식으로 전환하세요.
1. My girlfriend gave a present to me.
(나의 여자 친구는 나에게 선물 하나를 줬다.)
2. My dad made a chair for me.
(아빠는 나에게 의자를 만들어줬다.)
3. His mom cooks ramen for him.
(그의 엄마는 그에게 라면을 요리해준다.)
4. I built a small house for my son.
(나는 내 아들에게 작은 집을 지어줬다.)
5. They bought something special for me.
(그들은 나에게 특별한 무언가를 사줬다.)
6. You showed your love to her.
(당신은 그녀에게 당신의 사랑을 보였다.)
7. They sent a book to him.
(그들은 그에게 책 한 권을 보냈다.)

Exercise 1-1)
다음 3형식 문장을 4형식으로 전환하세요.
1. Lucas bought Jane a bicycle.
(Lucas는 Jane에게 자전거 한 대를 사줬다.)
2. I asked you a favor.
(나는 당신에게 부탁 하나를 했다.)
3. We found you a job.
(우리는 당신에게 일자리 하나를 찾아줬다.)
4. John sent his mom a letter.
(John은 그의 엄마에게 편지 하나를 보냈다.)
5. The waiter brought me an onion soup.
(웨이터가 나에게 양파스프를 가져다줬다.)

6. My mom gave me some cookies.
(엄마는 나에게 약간의 쿠키를 줬다.)

Exercise 2)

다음 주어진 문장을 영작하세요. (예시답안입니다.)
1. I bought him a wallet.
2. I asked my teacher a question.
3. He sent me the box.
4. I understand his poverty.
5. I had lunch.

Exercise 2-1)

다음 주어진 문장을 영작하세요. (예시답안입니다.)
1. Pass me the salt, please. (4형식)
2. I read the book. (3형식)
3. Jane told them a secret. (4형식)
4. I want a present. (3형식)
5. She lent me a watch. (4형식)

Unit 5 5형식

(1) 5형식 기본

Exercise 1)

괄호 안에서 올바른 문장의 형식을 선택하고 해석하세요.
1. (5형식) 나는 그의 조언이 쓸모없다는 것을 발견했다.
2. (5형식) 그는 그의 아들을 의사로 만들었다.
3. (5형식) 그들은 나를 미치게 만든다.
4. (4형식) 그는 어제 나에게 저녁을 사줬다.
5. (4형식) 나의 엄마는 나에게 케이크를 만들어줬다.
6. (5형식) 그들은 그를 회장으로 뽑았다.
7. (4형식) 그 선생님은 나에게 교과서 한 권을 사줬다.
8. (4형식) 그는 그녀에게 질문 하나를 했다.

Exercise 1-1)

괄호 안에서 올바른 문장의 형식을 선택하고 해석하세요.
1. (4형식) 나의 아빠는 나에게 그의 시계를 줬다.
2. (5형식) 그녀는 그를 수의사로 만들었다.

3. (5형식) 우리는 그녀를 Jane이라고 이름지어줬다.
4. (4형식) 나는 종종 그에게 웃기는 무언가를 보여준다.
5. (5형식) Susan은 그 책이 어렵다는 것을 발견했다.
6. (4형식) 그의 아버지는 그에게 엄청난 재산을 남길 것이다.
7. (4형식) Tom은 나에게 멋진 샌드위치를 만들어줬다.
8. (4형식) 우리는 그에게 고층빌딩 하나를 지어줬다.

(2) 5형식 응용

Exercise 1) 다음 주어진 문장을 해석하세요.
1. 선생님은 나에게 그 비밀을 말하라고 요구했다.
2. 나는 그녀에게 시험을 치라고 말했다.
3. 그들은 내가 그 동아리에 가입하기를 원한다.
4. 빌딩 안에 사람들은 누군가가 소녀에게 소리 지르는 것을 들었다.
5. 나는 그가 그녀를 만나도록 설득했다.
6. 그들은 사무실 안에서 무언가 타는 것을 냄새 맡았다.

Exercise 1-1) 다음 문장을 해석하세요.
1. 사람들은 그 사고를 비밀로 한다.
2. 그들은 새들이 나무에서 노래하는 것을 들었다.
3. 한 학생은 선생님이 그에게 숙제를 내주지 말 것을 요구했다.
4. 그들은 내가 이 차를 운전하길 원한다.
5. 그는 그의 룸메이트에게 방을 청소하라고 시켰다.

Exercise 2)

다음 문장을 문법에 맞게 고치고 해석하세요.
1. calling → to call (나는 곧 그가 나에게 전화를 주길 기대한다.)
2. went → go (나는 Tom이 도서관을 가게 만들 거야.)
3. to sing → sing(ing) (나는 그녀가 노래를 부르는 것을 보았다.)
4. come → to come (나는 그에게 여기로 오라고 말했다.)
5. go → to go (나는 그녀기 우리랑 같이 수영하러 갔으면 좋겠어.)
6. lending → to lend (책들 좀 빌려주실 수 있는지 여쭤도 될까요?)
7. to dancing → dance(dancing) (나는 그녀가 춤

추는 것을 보았다.)

8. to laugh → laugh (그녀는 사람들을 계속해서 웃게 만들었다.)

9. finish → to finish (나는 네가 이 일을 먼저 마치길 원해.)

10. to shouting → shout(ing) (그녀는 어떤 사람이 그녀에게 소리 지르는 것을 들었다.)

Exercise 2-1) 다음 문장을 문법적으로 옳게 고치세요.

1. finish → to finish (나는 John이 제때에 그 프로젝트를 마치길 기대한다.)

2. to play → play(ing) (우리는 그녀가 피아노를 연주하는 것을 들었다.)

3. to laugh → laugh(ing) (그들은 내가 크게 웃는 것을 봤다.)

4. did → do (그들은 내가 그것을 즉시 하도록 시켰다.)

5. to introduce → introduce (그가 그 자신을 소개하게 해.)

6. clean → to clean (Jane은 Tom이 그녀의 방을 청소하도록 요청했다.)

7. to hitting → hit(ting) (나는 누군가 나를 친다고 느꼈다.)

8. wash → to wash (나는 제인에게 설거지를 하라고 말했다.)

9. rang → ring(ing) (나는 전화기가 울리는 것을 들었다.)

10. teach → to teach (우리는 그 철학자가 우리에게 행복한 삶을 사는 방법을 가르쳐주도록 요청했다.)

Exercise 3)

다음 문장을 5형식 문장으로 영작하세요. (예시답안입니다.)

1. She watched her dog run(ning) fast.

2. I heard them sing(ing) in the house.

3. I will help you (to) study Korean.

4. He called himself a genius.

5. John found the movie attractive.

6. David told her to wash the dishes.

7. On my authority as chairman, I order you to leave this room.

8. He felt the anger rise(rising) in his body.

9. This bag helps me (to) carry heavy books.

Exercise 3-1)

다음 문장을 5형식 문장으로 영작하세요. (예시답안입니다.)

1. My mom made me clean my room.

2. They want me to join the team.

3. The doctor advised her to quit smoking.

4. I considered the idea very good.

5. I helped him (to) persuade Mac.

6. I saw a boy drink(ing) beer.

7. John heard birds sing(ing) peacefully.

8. I will never let him go.

▶ 단원 결합문제 (Unit 1-5) -본문 29 페이지

Exercise 1)

다음 문장들이 몇 형식 문장인지 밝히고 해석하세요.

1. (3형식) 그들은 영화를 봤다.

2. (2형식) 그녀는 화나 보인다.

3. (1형식) 그 요정은 사라졌다.

4. (2형식) 당신은 멋져 보인다.

5. (2형식) 그들은 좋은 친구들이다.

6. (4형식) 나는 나의 아내에게 새 반지를 사줬다.

7. (5형식) 나는 Sally가 거짓말쟁이라고 믿지 않는다.

8. (3형식) 제가 당신의 노트북을 사용해도 될까요?

9. (4형식) 나는 그녀에게 멋진 집 한 채를 찾아주었다.

10. (3형식) 나는 그녀의 멋진 집을 발견했다.

Exercise 1-1)

다음 문장들이 몇 형식 문장인지 밝히고 해석하세요.

1. (3형식) 나는 그 회의에 참석했다.

2. (5형식) 우리는 그녀를 Pretty라고 부른다.

3. (2형식) 이 초콜릿은 맛이 없다.

4. (1형식) 그는 무릎을 꿇었다.

5. (3형식) 아무것도 내가 나의 의무를 이행하는 것을 막을 수 없다.

6. (3형식) 그 아이들은 강아지를 좋아한다.

7. (5형식) 나는 그를 멍청이라고 여긴다.

8. (2형식) 그녀의 계획은 훌륭하게 들린다.

9. (4형식) 당신은 나에게 스페인어를 일주일에 세 번 가르쳐주실 수 있나요?

10. (2형식) 우리의 꿈은 많은 점에서 이루어졌다.

Exercise 1-2)

다음 문장들이 몇 형식 문장인지 밝히고 해석하세요.

1. (2형식) 그 낯선 사람은 매우 친절했다.

2. (1형식) 많은 사람들이 건물 안에 있다.

3. (1형식) 많은 기자들이 모였다.

4. (2형식) 그 집은 변하지 않은 채로 있다.

5. (2형식) 이 상황은 거의 이해할 수 없다.

6. (1형식) 이 시계는 전혀 작동하지 않는다.

7. (3형식) 그녀는 몇몇의 식물을 키웠다.

8. (2형식) 그녀는 그와 불쾌하다고 느꼈다.

9. (3형식) 나는 종종 그에게 거짓말을 한다.

10. (5형식) 그녀의 변명이 나를 화나게 만들었다.

Unit 6 감탄문

(1) What+a+형용사+명사 (+주어+동사)!

(2) How+형용사/부사 (+주어+동사)!

Exercise 1)

다음 문장을 How로 시작하는 감탄문으로 바꾸세요.

1. How kind (she is)!

2. How tall (Tom is)!

3. How expensive (the car is)!

4. How smart (John is)!

5. How rich (Jane is)!

Exercise 1-1)

다음 문장을 What으로 시작하는 감탄문으로 바꾸세요.

1. What a famous actor! (he is)

2. What a luxury bag! (she bought)

3. What a wonderful thing! (you did)

4. What good friends! (we are)

5. What a gorgeous house! (Sean built)

■ 단원별 문제 -본문 35 페이지

Chapter 1. 문장의 구성

Unit 1-6

1. ④

tip!

④는 형용사, 나머지는 부사

2. ③

tip!

sadly → sad: ③에 쓰인 look은 2형식으로 쓰였다. look이 2형식에 쓰일 경우 뒤에 형용사가 오는데 sadly는 부사이기 때문에 형용사인 sad로 바꿔줘야 한다.

3. ④

tip!

①~⑤ 모두 2형식 문장이다. 2형식 동사 중에서도 감각동사 뒤에는 형용사가 오는데 ④번을 제외한 나머지는 모두 부사가 왔다.

따라서 ① excitingly → exciting ② weirdly → weird ③ softly → soft ⑤ wonderfully → wonderful 로 바꿔줘야 맞는 문장이 된다.

4. ③

tip!

보기의 단어들은 모두 4형식 동사이나 ③을 제외한 나머지는 3형식으로 전환할 때 전치사 to를 사용하는 동사들이기 때문에 보기에 적절하다. ③은 3형식으로 전환할 때 전치사 for을 사용한다.

5. to

tip!

give와 teach는 모두 3형식으로 전환할 때 전치사 to를 사용한다.

6. ①

tip!

①번을 제외한 나머지는 사역동사('시키다'의 의미)로 쓰였기 때문에 동사 뒤에 동사원형이 나왔지만 ①번은 '가지다'의 의미의 3형식 동사이다.
① 그는 그의 방에 컴퓨터를 가지고 있었다.
② 그는 그의 남자형제가 그 책을 읽게 했다.
③ 그는 그 학생이 교실을 청소하게 했다.
④ 그는 그의 아내가 그들을 위해 저녁을 준비하게 했다.
⑤ 그는 우리가 모든 쓰레기를 치우게 했다.

7. ②
tip!
want는 사역동사도, 지각동사도 아니기 때문에 뒤에 to부정사가 온다. 또한 to부정사 뒤에는 동사원형을 쓴다.

8. ④
tip!
④번은 3형식이고 나머지는 2형식이다.

9. ④
tip!
주어진 문장은 간접목적어, 직접목적어가 있는 4형식 문장이기 때문에 4형식 동사인 lend가 적절하다.
• lent : 빌려주다
• borrow: 빌리다

10. (1) 1형식: 그녀는 갑자기 나타났다.
    (2) 2형식: 그녀는 약한 것처럼 보인다.

11. ⑤
tip!
⑤번은 목적보어이며 나머지는 목적어이다.

12. ③
tip!
다음 주어진 문장은 2형식 문장 중에서도 감각동사가 쓰인 문장이므로 동사 뒤에 형용사가 나와야 하는데 ③번만 부사이다.

13. ①
tip!
보기에 주어진 두 문장에 모두 지각동사가 쓰였기 때문에 동사원형이나 동사+ing 형태가 빈칸에 적절한데 이 두 가지를 모두 충족시키는 것은 ①번밖에 없다.

14. How interesting
15. What a nice
16. ③
tip!
문장에 본동사 뒤에 있는 relax가 원형이기 때문에 사역동사나 지각동사가 올 수 있다. 해당사항 없는 get이 답이 된다.

17. ②
tip!
make는 사역동사이기 때문에 동사원형이 와야 한다. 따라서 to clean → clean

18. ②
tip!
②번에 쓴 want는 지각동사도 사역동사도 아니기 때문에 뒤에 to부정사가 와야 한다. 따라서 take → to take

19. ①
tip!
①번은 직접목적어이며 그 외 나머지는 모두 보어이다.

20. ④
tip!
sound는 2형식 동사 중에서도 감각동사이기 때문에 뒤에 형용사가 보어로 와야 하는데 ④번은 부사이다.

21. 1 found the bag heavy.
22. ③
tip!
③번은 3형식 문장이며 나머지는 모두 4형식 문장이다.

23. ②
tip!
②번은 How가 적절하며 나머지는 모두 What이 적절하다.

24. play 또는 playing
25. to visit

Chapter 2 시제

Unit 7 현재와 현재진행

(1) 동사의 -ing형 만들기
Exercise 1) 다음 주어진 동사들의 +ing를 쓰세요.
1. eating
2. making
3. laying
4. buying
5. sleeping
6. carrying
7. selling
8. understanding
9. having
10. jogging
11. borrowing
12. telling
13. fighting
14. listening

Exercise 1-1) 다음 주어진 동사들의 +ing를 쓰세요.
1. dreaming
2. loving
3. putting
4. losing
5. living
6. shutting
7. lending
8. hearing
9. swimming
10. walking
11. drinking
12. singing
13. shopping
14. passing

Exercise 2) 다음 문장을 현재 진행형으로 바꾸세요.
1. She is telling the story to us.
2. I am buying some shirts.
3. Bob is speaking loudly.
4. The birds are singing a song.
5. John is falling asleep.
6. She is shopping in the department store.
7. It is raining.
8. They are studying math.
9. He is dancing on the floor.
10. She is playing the guitar.

Exercise 2-1) 다음 문장을 현재시제로 바꾸세요.
1. We buy some food.
2. They run fast.
3. Sally listens to the music.
4. I swim in the ocean.
5. Sean drives to his home.
6. We sing a song.
7. She laughs loudly.
8. He spends too much money.
9. The ring shines in the dark.
10. They change colors.

(2) 현재와 현재진행형의 비교
Exercise 1)
다음 괄호 안에서 적절한 표현을 고르세요.
1. plays (그녀는 주말마다 바이올린을 연주한다.)
2. exist (유니콘은 실제로 존재한다.)
3. don't like (그들은 그녀를 좋아하지 않는다.)
4. is playing (그녀는 지금 축구를 하고 있다.)
5. looks (그는 슬퍼 보인다.)
6. go (학생들은 매일 학교에 간다.)
7. has (그녀는 고양이 한 마리를 가지고 있다.)
8. is boiling (그 주전자를 지금 끓고 있다.)
9. boils (물은 100도에서 끓는다.)
10. always make (그들은 항상 나를 행복하게 만든다.)

Exercise 1-1)

다음 괄호 안에서 적절한 표현을 고르세요.

1. fight (그들은 때때로 서로 싸운다.)
2. is (그 생물체는 그 호수 안에 살아있다.)
3. lives (그녀는 도쿄에 산다.)
4. tells (그는 결코 거짓말을 하지 않는다.)
5. is telling (그는 외출금지 당하지 않으려고 지금은 거짓말을 하고 있다.)
6. smells (그 향수는 장미 같은 향이 난다.)
7. cries (그녀는 종종 심하게 운다.)
8. studies (그는 매일 공부한다.)
9. is studying (그는 지금 영어를 공부하고 있는 중이다.)
10. give (그들은 나에게 월요일마다 꽃다발을 준다.)

Exercise 2)

다음 문장을 영작하세요. (예시답안입니다.)

1. I am taking a nap now.
2. I take a nap every day.
3. We go to church every Sunday morning.
4. Poly always gets up early in the morning.
5. The sun rises in the east.

Exercise 2-1)

다음 문장을 영작하세요. (예시답안입니다.)

1. I am studying hard at home.
2. I study hard every day.
3. We are playing soccer.
4. We play soccer every Sunday.
5. They are having dinner.

Unit 8 과거와 과거진행

(1) 과거

Exercise 1)

다음 주어진 단어들의 과거형을 쓰세요.

1. rob - robbed

2. agree - agreed
3. marry - married
4. hope - hoped
5. love - loved
6. carry - carried
7. clean - cleaned
8. plan - planned
9. hurry - hurried
10. offer - offered
11. call - called
12. die - died
13. enjoy - enjoyed
14. end - ended

Exercise 1-1)

다음 주어진 단어들의 과거형을 쓰세요.

1. stop - stopped
2. climb - climbed
3. beg - begged
4. talk - talked
5. close - closed
6. change - changed
7. study - studied
8. fly - flew/flied
9. drop - dropped
10. admit - admitted
11. occur - occurred
12. fry - fried
13. play - played
14. turn - turned

(2) 과거진행

Exercise 1)

다음 주어진 문장을 과거 진행형으로 바꾸세요.

1. I was having lunch.
2. I was taking a bath.
3. I was calling you.
4. She was studying hard.
5. We were going to the movies.

6. He was reading a novel.

7. I was singing a song in the concert hall.

8. She was cutting the paper into stars.

9. He was stealing the bread.

10. I was drawing the picture.

Exercise 1-1)

다음 주어진 문장을 단순과거형으로 바꾸세요.

1. My dad washed the dishes.

2. We had dinner.

3. They ran away from home.

4. I took a shower.

5. She went for a swim.

6. He spread the rumor.

7. I clicked the button.

8. We fought with the bullies.

9. He kicked the boxes.

10. They drove along the new highway.

Exercise 2)

다음 주어진 문장을 참고해서 빈칸을 채우세요.

1. I was sleeping.

2. I was talking too much,

3. you were playing the computer game,

4. He was bothering me

5. I was running a marathon.

Exercise 3) 다음 문장을 영작하세요. (예시답안입니다.)

1. I was walking in the rain.

2. It was raining hard outside when he came back.

3. When I was swimming in the pool, I lost the key.

4. Someone broke in when I was cooking.

5. She was carrying a bag under her arm.

6. She dried her hair in front of the fan.

7. They ate pizza at my house yesterday.

Exercise 3-1) 다음 문장을 영작하세요. (예시답안입니다.)

1. We walked to school.

2. He played soccer with his friends.

3. I was sleeping when you called me.

4. Jane was watching TV in the living room.

5. We studied English hard.

6. They were doing the dishes.

7. Tom was singing when I came in.

Unit 9 미래

(1) 미래를 나타내는 조동사 will

(2) be going to 동사원형

Exercise 1)

다음 문장을 보기와 같이 바꾸세요.

1. She is going to come again.

2. He is going to ask for his friend.

3. I am going to eat later.

4. We are going to go to the movies tonight.

5. John is going to be an athlete.

6. Sooner or later, you are going to agree with me.

Exercise 1-1) 다음 문장을 보기와 같이 바꾸세요.

1. They will join the club.

2. We will study in a group.

3. He will call me tomorrow.

4. I will go swimming tonight.

5. Will you be a teacher?

6. Everything will fall into place.

Exercise 2) 다음 주어진 문장을 영작하세요. (예시답안입니다.)

1. I will work at this company.

2. She will call me.

3. We will have dinner together.

4. Tom won't(will not) go to school tomorrow.

5. It will rain tomorrow.

Exercise 2-1) 다음 주어진 문장을 영작하세요. (예시 답안입니다)

1. I will go abroad.
2. She will sell her house.
3. They will rent a car.
4. He will be a soccer player.
5. I will never call you again.

Unit 10 현재완료

(1) 과거분사 형태 만들기

Exercise 1) 다음 주어진 단어들의 과거분사형을 쓰세요.

1. rob - robbed
2. agree - agreed
3. marry - married
4. hope - hoped
5. love - loved
6. change - changed
7. study - studied
8. fly - flown/flied
9. drop - dropped
10. admit - admitted
11. occur - occurred
12. fry - fried
13. play - played
14. turn - turned

Exercise 1-1) 다음 주어진 단어들의 과거형을 쓰세요.

1. stop - stopped
2. climb - climbed
3. beg - begged
4. talk - talked
5. close - closed
6. carry - carried
7. clean - cleaned
8. plan - planned
9. hurry - hurried

10. offer - offered
11. call - called
12. die - died
13. enjoy - enjoyed
14. end - ended

Exercise 2)
다음 문장을 현재완료형 문장으로 바꾸세요.

1. I have worked in this company.
2. Jane hasn't (has not) slept.
3. I have seen a movie.
4. I have gone to Japan.
5. They have lived in Korea.
6. Five years have passed.
7. This program has invited you to Busan.
8. We have studied together since we were very young.
9. We have kept in touch with each other for a long time.
10. She has driven to Incheon.

Exercise 2-1)
다음 문장을 현재완료형 문장으로 바꾸세요.

1. I have cleaned my room.
2. My mom hasn't(has not) cooked dinner for us.
3. He has gone to the park.
4. The bus has already left.
5. We haven't(have not) known each other.
6. She has helped someone twice in her life.
7. Jane hasn't(has not) done volunteer work.
8. The milk has already gone bad.
9. The task hasn't(has not) been stressful for me.
10. We have had dinner together.

(2) 현재완료의 용법

Exercise 1)
괄호 안의 단어들을 활용하여 현재완료형 문장으로 영작하고 용법도 구별하세요. (예시답안입니다.)

1. I have met him before. (경험)

2. We haven't(have not) had dinner yet. (완료)

3. I have worked at this company since 3 years ago. (계속)

4. The train has just left. (완료)

5. She has already seen the movie. (완료)

6. I have never seen that sort of car before. (경험)

Exercise 1-1)

괄호 안의 단어들을 활용하여 현재완료형 문장으로 영작하세요. (예시답안입니다.)

1. I have been to China twice.

2. I haven't finished my homework yet.

3. I have never met the actor.

4. The plane has just arrived.

5. I have already been there.

6. Jack has been there once.

Unit 11 과거와 현재완료

Exercise 1)

다음 괄호 안에서 적절한 단어를 고르세요.

1. yesterday

2. three years ago

3. saw

4. has worked

5. before

Exercise 1-1)

다음 괄호 안에서 적절한 단어를 고르세요.

1. has been

2. went

3. provided

4. finished

5. for 10 years

■ 단원별 문제 -본문 72 페이지

Chapter 2. 시제
Unit 7-11

1. ②
tip!
finds → find
2. ①
tip!
'가지다'라는 의미의 have를 진행형으로 쓰지는 않는다.
3. ④
① I'm knowing → I have known
② She is possessing → She possesses
③ I'm believing → I believe
⑤ This mansion is belonging → This mansion belongs
4. is rushing
5. was raining
6. ③
tip!
③ find-found-found
7. ④
tip!
④ drive-drove-driven
8. ④
tip!
④ Tom은 미국으로 가버렸다. (그래서 지금 없다)
9. ④
10. (1) Tom hasn't(has not) fixed his car.
   (2) Has Jack watched TV?
11. ⑤
12. was studying for
13. was taking a rest
14. have you had, hurt, was carrying
15. ④
tip!
① in 1998 → 과거시제와 사용

② last week → 과거시제와 사용
③ next month → 미래시제와 사용
⑤ yesterday → 과거시제와 사용
16. ④
17. ⑤
tip!
보기는 현재완료의 계속적 용법이다.
18. ③
tip!
③은 미래부사어구이다.
19. hasn't(has not) done
tip!
since then은 '그때 이후로/이래로'로 해석되며
현재완료시제와 어울린다.
20. ⑤
tip!
⑤을 제외한 보기들은 진행형으로 잘 쓰지 않는 경우
이다.
21. (1) has gone (가버렸다, 가고 없다)
    (2) has been (가본 적이 있다)
22. have objected
tip!
나는 그 사고 이래로 지금까지 아이들이 늦게까지
머무르게 하는 것을 반대해오고 있다.
23. ③
tip!
모두 현재완료시제를 사용했지만 현재완료 중에
서도 ③은 완료 용법을, 나머지 전부는 경험 용법
을 사용했다.
24. ②
tip!
보기에 쓰인 현재완료시제는 경험 용법이다.
25. ③
tip!
③ lived → have lived

Chapter 3 조동사

Unit 12 can, may, will

(1) 허락과 허가의 조동사 can, may

(2) 능력의 조동사 can

(3) 추측의 조동사 may

(4) 미래의 조동사 will

(5) 의지의 조동사 will

Exercise 1)

다음 문장을 해석하세요.
1. 내 심장은 계속 뛸 것이다.
2. 수요일에 날씨가 어떨 것 같나요?
3. 부탁 하나만 해도 될까요?
4. 함께 모이는 거 괜찮을까요?
5. 우리들 사진을 좀 찍어줄 수 있나요?
6. 당신은 나를 위해서 무엇을 해줄 수 있나요?
7. 몇몇 사람들은 당신에게 쿠키를 줄 것이다.
8. 나중에 전화 걸어도 될까요?
9. 당신은 불어를 할 수 있나요?

Exercise 1-1)

다음 문장을 해석하세요.
1. 언젠가 그녀는 돌아올 것이다.
2. 그 개인 비행기는 당신을 만족시킬 것이다.
3. 우리는 폐기물을 재활용함으로써 온실가스들을 줄
일 수 있다.
4. 그는 혼자서 그 문제를 해결할 수 없다.
5. 메시지 하나 남길 수 있을까요?
6. 우리는 장난감들을 가지고 놀 것이다.
7. 시간이 지날수록 나의 삶은 쉬워지고, 행복해질 것
이다.

Exercise 2)

다음 조동사 can, may, will의 용법으로 알맞은 것에
O표 하세요.
1. 허가 (제가 지금 떠나도 될까요?)
2. 능력, 가능 (당신은 독일어를 할 수 있나요?)

3. 의지미래 (나는 최선을 다할 것이다.)

4. 추측 (이 책은 당신에게 도움이 될지도 모른다.)

5. 능력, 가능 (그들은 선생님 없이 그 문제들을 해결할 수 있다.)

6. 추측 (그녀는 어쩌면 진실을 알지도 모른다. 내가 그녀에게 물어보겠다.)

7. 허가 (당신은 과제를 끝났다면 그와 외출해도 좋다.)

8. 허가 (제가 당신을 도와드릴까요?)

9. 능력, 가능 (나는 당장은 방을 청소할 수 없다.)

Exercise 2-1)

다음 조동사 can, may, will의 용법으로 알맞은 것에 O표 하세요.

1. 허가 (제가 이 펜으로 편지를 써도 될까요?)

2. 능력, 가능 (그녀는 혼자서 그 문을 열 수 있다.)

3. 단순미래 (곧 어두워질 것이다.)

4. 허가 (당신은 지금 가도 좋다.)

5. 허가 (제가 당신의 노트북을 써도 될까요?)

6. 능력, 가능 (당신은 물고기보다 더 빠르게 수영할 수 있나요?)

7. 의지미래 (나는 혼자서 이 문제를 해결할 것이다.)

8. 추측 (이 소식은 어쩌면 사실이 아닐지도 모른다.)

Exercise 3)

같은 의미의 문장이 되도록 괄호 안에 적절한 단어를 쓰세요.

1. is able to

2. Are able to

3. can not

4. can

5. am going to

Exercise 3-1)

같은 의미의 문장이 되도록 괄호 안에 적절한 단어를 쓰세요.

1. is able to

2. are not able to

3. is going to

4. will

5. am not able to

Exercise 4)

다음 주어진 문장을 영작하세요. (예시답안입니다.)

1. Can you speak English?

2. May(can) I help you?

3. I will do my best.

4. May(can) I write a letter with this pencil?

5. This movie may be fun to them.

6. She can run fast.

7. Can you come here tomorrow?

8. Can you fully understand my lecture?

9. He will buy a smart phone someday.

Exercise 4-1)

다음 주어진 문장을 영작하세요. (예시답안입니다.)

1. I can't speak Spanish.

2. This movie may be boring to you.

3. Will you come here tomorrow?

4. May(Can) I use your dictionary?

5. Can you protect this area alone?

6. Kate will be thirty next year.

7. You may(can) go home now.

8. I will never do it again.

9. He will control his emotion.

본문 83 페이지

Unit 13 must, have to, should

(1) must

(2) have to

(3) should (=ought to)

(4) must와 should, have to의 부정문

Exercise 1)

다음 문장의 의미가 비슷하도록 빈칸을 채우세요.

1. have to
2. ought to
3. must
4. has to
5. ought to

Exercise 1-1)

다음 문장의 의미가 비슷하도록 빈칸을 채우세요.

1. have to
2. ought to
3. has to
4. ought to
5. should

Exercise 2)

다음 문장에서 must의 용법으로 적절한 것에 O표 하세요.

1. 강한 추측 (그녀는 외국인임에 틀림없다.)
2. 필요, 의무 (당신은 허가 없이 거기에 가서는 안 된다.)
3. 필요, 의무 (그는 그의 선생님을 존경해야 한다.)
4. 강한 추측 (그녀는 나 때문에 많이 화났음에 틀림없다.)
5. 강한 추측 (당신은 농담을 하고 있음에 틀림없다.)
6. 강한 추측 (당신은 이맘때쯤이면 향수병에 걸릴 것임에 틀림없다.)
7. 필요, 의무 (우리는 최선을 다해야만 한다.)
8. 필요, 의무 (그녀는 즉시 그녀의 일을 해야만 한다.)
9. 강한 추측 (Tom은 너무 잘생겼기 때문에 학교에서 인기 있음에 틀림없어.)
10. 필요, 의무 (사람은 땀 흘려 일하면서 살아야만 한다.)

Exercise 3)

다음 문장을 단순히 부정문으로 바꾸고 그에 맞게 해석하세요.

1.
→ You don't have to work at the factory.
→ 너는 그 공장에서 일할 필요가 없다.

2.
→ We should not grab the chances.
→ 우리는 그 기회들을 잡지 말아야 한다.

3.
→ She must not clean her room.
→ 그녀는 그녀의 방을 치워서는 안 된다.

4.
→ We must not follow his direction.
→ 우리는 그의 방향을 따라서는 안 된다.

5.
→ I shouldn't feed my cat.
→ 나는 나의 고양이에게 먹이를 주지 말아야 한다.

Exercise 3-1)

다음 문장을 단순히 부정문으로 바꾸고 그에 맞게 해석하세요.

1.
→ You must not increase the sales of the company.
→ 너는 회사의 판매를 늘려서는 안 된다.

2.
→ You don't have to tell me everything about Jane.
→ 너는 Jane에 관한 모든 것을 나에게 말 할 필요는 없다.

3.
→ We should not listen to them carefully.
→ 우리는 그들의 말을 신중히 듣지 않아야 한다.

4.
→ We ought not to speak in English here.
→ 우리는 여기서 영어를 쓰지 말아야 한다.

5.
→ They must not finish the project as soon as possible.
→ 우리는 이 프로젝트를 가능한 빨리 끝내서는 안 된다.

Unit 14 used to, would

(1) used to

(2) would

Exercise 1)

다음 문장을 영작하세요. (예시답안입니다.)

1. I used to live in Japan.
2. I used to stay (at) home every Sunday.
3. I would sometimes play soccer with friends.
4. He would often get up late in the morning.
5. There used to be a tall building over there.

Exercise 1-1)

다음 문장을 영작하세요. (예시답안입니다.)

1. I would sing a song alone in the room.
2. He used to call them every Saturday.
3. He used to take a shower every evening.
4. I used to live with my family.

3. Can you share the bread with him?
4. He will trust her.
5. May I use your dictionary?
6. You should follow the rules.
7. Should I read this book?
8. Can I advertise the product?
9. I can climb up the tree.

Exercise 1-3)

다음 문장을 영작하세요. (예시답안입니다.)

1. Kate will graduate from high school next year.
2. May I write a letter with a pencil?
3. Will you come here tomorrow?
4. Did you go to the party yesterday?
5. Can(May) we overcome the crisis?
6. I will never do that again.
7. You should prepare for the mid-term exam.
8. You should not eat too much.

▶ **단원 결합문제 (Unit 12-14)** -본문 96 페이지

Exercise 1)

다음 문장을 영작하세요. (예시답안입니다.)

1. You should say hello to her.
2. You have to do it right now.
3. He must be younger than me.
4. You don't have to read this book.
5. Can(May) I write this letter with this pen?
6. Do I have to go there tomorrow?
7. You shouldn't drink alcohol too much.
8. You have to call Jane right now.

Exercise 1-2)

다음 문장을 영작하세요. (예시답안입니다.)

1. She has to walk all day.
2. He can enter the room without permission.

■ 단원별 문제 -본문 99 페이지

Chapter 3. 조동사

Unit 12-14

1. ⑤
tip!
나는 다이어트를 할 거야. 나는 저녁에 8시 이후에
먹지 않을거야.

2. plays → play
tip!
조동사 바로 다음에는 동사원형이 온다.

3. ②
tip!
조동사 다음에는 동사원형을 써야한다.

4. ④

5. ⑤
tip!
나는 우유 좀 사러 식료품점에 갈지도 몰라.
보기의 may는 '~일지도 모른다.'의 추측을 나타
내고 있고 ⑤번도 그렇다. 나머지는 허락/허가의
may이다.

6. ①

7. can't be

8. ①
tip!
② speaks → speak
③ 조동사 2개를 한 번에 사용할 수 없다.
④ yesterday는 과거시제와 사용
⑤ don't able to → am not able to

9. ③
tip!
해석이 어색(must가 더 잘 어울림).

10. will have to

11. ③

12. ①
tip!
①은 '임에 틀림없다'로 해석되는 추측의 조동사
must이며 나머지는 '해야 한다'로 해석되는 의무
의 조동사로 쓰였다.

13. C(c)an

14. used to
tip!
used to + 동사원형: 예전에 ~했었다.

15. doesn't have to(=doesn't need to)

16. ①
A:티켓을 사기위해 줄을 설게.
B:우리 줄 설 필요 없어. 내가 이미 우리 티켓을
예약해놨거든.

17. can

18. May

19. ②

20. ①

Chapter 4 수동태

Unit 15 수동태

(1) 능동태와 수동태

(2) 「by 행위자」의 생략

(3) 수동태의 시제

*부사(전치사+명사)의 위치는 유연하게

Exercise 1)

다음 주어진 능동태 문장을 수동태로 바꾸세요. (현재시제)

1. He is loved by them.
2. The tiger is led by the little mouse.
3. English is spoken by Americans.
4. A tree is grown by my grandmother.
5. The piano is played by the birds.
6. The garden is cleaned by him every day.
7. Windows are broken by them.
8. The machine is used by him effectively.
9. Water is absorbed by a sponge.
10. Her every task is delayed by Poly.

Exercise 1-1)

다음 주어진 능동태 문장을 수동태로 바꾸세요.
(과거, 조동사)

1. The novel was written by Kim in 1993.
2. A hamburger will be eaten by her.
3. The barrier was broken by them.
4. The bike can be fixed by her sister.
5. The roses were sold by them at a low price.
6. The coffee was served by her.
7. This building was built by him in 2001.
8. Hanguel was invented by King Sejong.
9. The paper will be cut by her.
10. The wall was painted by Kelly.

Exercise 1-2)

다음 주어진 능동태 문장을 수동태로 바꾸세요. (종합)

1. The town was attacked by the army at dawn.

2. Lots of books will be bought by them.
3. A cute cat is raised by her.
4. A building was built by John.
5. The expensive car can be bought by us.
6. The report should be finished by Brad within this week.
7. My decision was changed by me yesterday.
8. The door will be fixed by us today.
9. Cookies are sold by them on the street.
10. The machine will be broken by Susan.

Exercise 2)

다음 수동태 문장들은 능동태로, 능동태는 수동태로 바꾸세요.

1. A book is written by Tom.
2. She can solve the problem.
3. All the apples were eaten by him.
4. Tom teaches Jane.
5. This movie will be directed by Mr. Yang.
6. The violin was played by Sophie.
7. My mom doesn't clean my room.
8. The yard is cleaned by me every day.
9. A school was founded by Minsu.
10. Her cup was broken by John.

Exercise 2-1)

다음 수동태 문장들은 능동태로, 능동태는 수동태로 바꾸세요.

1. My watch was stolen by somebody.
2. The floor is cleaned by them every Monday.
3. Tom broke the vase.
4. The teacher cancels the class.
5. Many people use the Internet nowadays.
6. This rule should be obeyed by you.
7. The Mona Lisa was painted by Da Vinci.
8. Stars in the sky can be seen by us.
9. Sally wasn't invited to the party by him.
10. They sell the cars at a high price.

Exercise 3) 다음 괄호 안에 옳은 형태에 O표 하세요.

1. me
2. whom
3. isn't
4. made
5. was

Exercise 3-1) 다음 괄호 안에 옳은 형태에 O표 하세요.

1. Yes, it is.
2. written
3. locked
4. knew
5. painted

Exercise 4)

다음 주어진 단어를 활용해서 문장을 영작하세요.

1. I was hit by you.
2. He was placed in a separate room by the teacher.
3. The method was found by him.
4. Telephone was invented by Alexander Bell.
5. The bridge was built on the river.
6. This novel was written by Tom.

Exercise 4-1)

다음 주어진 단어를 활용해서 문장을 영작하세요.

1. These songs are sung by JYS.
2. By whom was this table made?
3. The singer is known to everyone.
4. You will be destroyed by rage.
5. These sneakers are made in Japan.
6. This classroom is cleaned by her every day.

Unit 16 수동태의 여러 형태

(1) 4형식과 5형식의 수동태

Exercise 1)

다음 문장을 수동태로 바꾸세요. (정답이 한 개일 수도 있음)

1.
→ We were showed(shown) a beautiful vase by Minji.
→ A beautiful vase was showed(shown) to us by Minji.

2.
→ X
→ A watch was bought for him by her.

3.
→ I was sent a present by them.
→ A present was sent to me by them.

4.
→ He was made sad by us.
→ X
tip! 원 문장이 목적어가 하나인 5형식이기 때문에 수동태로 한 문장만 가능하다.

5.
→ He was asked a question by me.
→ A question was asked of him by me.

Exercise 1-1)

다음 문장을 수동태로 바꾸세요. (정답이 한 개일 수도 있음)

1.
→ I am called Jane by Kim.
→ X
tip! 원 문장이 목적어가 하나인 5형식이기 때문에 수동태로 한 문장만 가능하다.

2.
→ X
→ Spaghetti is sometimes made for me by him.

3.
→ Children are taught Japanese by him.
→ Japanese is taught to children by him.

만 111 페이지

4.
→ He was got(gotten) a smartphone by Suzy.
→ A smartphone was got(gotten) for him by Suzy.
5.
→ She was got(gotten) upset by you.
→ X

tip! 원 문장이 목적어가 하나인 5형식이기 때문에 수동태로 한 문장만 가능하다.

(2) by 이외의 전치사를 사용하는 수동태
Exercise 1)
다음 괄호 안에 적절한 단어에 O표 하세요.

1. about
2. with
3. with
4. with
5. of
6. to
7. in
8. of
9. at
10. in

Exercise 2)
다음 빈칸을 주어진 단어를 활용하여 채우세요.

1. am worried about
2. is known as
3. is known to
4 am tired of
5. is satisfied with
6. Are, interested in
7. was involved in
8. was filled of (with)
9. be pleased with
10. was crowded with

■ 단원별 문제 -본문 120 페이지

Chapter 4. 수동태
Unit 15-16

1. ③
2. ②
3. ④
4. (1) feeds
   (2) is fed
5. with
6. from
 • make of: 물질적 변화로 재료의 성질이나 형태는 변하지 않을 때
 • make from: 화학적 변화로 재료의 성질이나 형태가 완전히 바뀌었을 때
7. ③
8. ③
9. stole → stolen
10. love → loved
11. ④
tip!
This road built → This road was built
12. ④
tip!
The cereals made → were/are/will be made 등 be p.p.의 구조로 써줘야 한다.
13. runs
14. was brought
15. passed (내 집을 지나쳤다.)
tip!
 • passed by: 지나치다
16. are used
17. am called
18. ④
19. ①
20. ④
21. ③
22. ④

23. ⑤

tip!

ⓑ Was the question understood by everyone?

ⓒ Black pepper was not discovered by american.

ⓓ Her homework may not be finished by her.

24. ⑤

tip!

⑤ → Where was this artifact found by you?

25.

(1) Lots of stars can be seen by us at night.

(2) Water was drunk by my sister after jogging.

Chapter 5 to부정사

Unit 17 to부정사의 명사적 용법

(1) 주어 역할

(2) 보어 역할

(3) 목적어 역할

Exercise 1)

다음 주어진 문장을 문법에 맞게 고치세요.

1. Study → To study (수학을 공부하는 것은 쉽지 않다.)
2. collect → to collect (나의 취미는 우표를 모으는 것이다.)
3. cook → to cook (그녀는 요리하는 것을 좋아한다.)
4. Be → To be (의사가 되는 것은 어렵다.)
5. take → to take (임무는 그녀의 사진을 찍는 것이었다.)
6. make → to make (나는 그와 화해하길 원한다.)
7. Stay → To stay (건강을 유지하는 것이 중요하다.)
8. Tell → To tell (거짓말을 하는 것은 관계에 있어서 최악이다.)
9. Get → To get (아침에 일찍 일어나는 것이 도움이 된다.)
10. Eat → To eat (하루에 사과 한 개씩 먹는 것이 너를 건강하게 유지해준다.)

Exercise 1-1)

다음 주어진 문장을 문법에 맞게 고치세요.

1. meet → to meet (나는 그녀를 다시 만나기로 결심했다.)
2. be → to be (나의 꿈은 치과의사가 되는 것이다.)
3. drink → to drink (그는 갈증이 났기 때문에 물을 마시기 위해 멈췄다.)
4. take → to take (그의 취미는 사진을 찍는 것이다.)
5. Swim → To swim (빠르게 수영하는 것이 그의 목표이다.)
6. do → to do (나는 그것을 무료로 할 것이라고 예상하지 않는다.)
7. leave → to leave (우리는 오늘밤 몰래 이 빌딩을 떠날 것을 계획했다.)

8. meet → to meet (나는 가능한 빨리 그녀를 만나기를 희망한다.)
9. Choose → To choose (좋은 책들을 고르는 것은 아이들에게 매우 중요하다.)
10. Meet → To meet (그녀를 만나는 것은 나를 행복하게 만든다.)

Exercise 2)

다음 문장을 진주어/가주어 문장으로 바꾸세요.
1. It is so stressful to watch three movies a day.
2. It is not easy for her to make a new friend.
3. It is bad for your health to play too long in the sun.
4. It makes you peaceful to take a stroll with a dog.
5. It is not easy to meet people like her.

Exercise 2-1)

다음 문장을 진주어/가주어 문장으로 바꾸세요.
1. To play computer games together is fun.
2. To meet you in another country was wonderful.
3. To keep pets is not easy.
4. To follow his instructions is very important.
5. To eat hamburgers every day is unhealthy.

Exercise 3)

주어진 단어를 활용하고 to 부정사를 이용하여 영작하세요.
1. To do your best is important.
   (= It is important to do your best.)
2. I want to go home and sleep.
3. My plan is to get on the first train.
4. I need to eat less.
5. To help one another is necessary.
   (= It is necessary to help one another.)
6. Justin began to lose weight.
7. I hope to visit the street one day.

Exercise 3-1)

주어진 단어를 활용하고 to 부정사를 이용하여 영작하세요.
1. My hobby is to see movies.
2. To get up early in the morning is good for

health.
   (= It is good for health to get up early in the morning.)
3. I decided to meet her tomorrow.
4. I want to drink something cold.
5. To become a singer is my dream.
6. We decided to take a risk.

Unit 18 의문사 + to부정사
Exercise 1)

다음 주어진 문장을 참고해서 빈칸을 채우세요.
1. where to meet
2. how to cook
3. how to open
4. where to start
5. how to play

Exercise 1-1)

다음 주어진 문장을 참고해서 빈칸을 채우세요.
1. how to go
2. when to start
3. what to cook
4. when to start
5. how to put

Unit 19 to부정사의 형용사적 용법
(1) to 부정사의 형용사적 용법이 가지는 특징
Exercise 1)

다음 문장을 문법에 맞게 고치고 해석하세요.
1. drink → to drink
→ (부탁해요, 마실 것을 저에게 주세요.)
2. say → to say
→ (그녀는 그렇게 말 할 소녀가 아니다.)
3. wear → to wear
→ (그는 입을 한 벌의 바지를 원한다.)

4. take → to take
→ (나는 여행기간 동안 복용할 약들을 샀다.)
5. solve → to solve
→ (그 문제를 해결할 정답이 있을 것이다.)
6. persuade → to persuade
→ (이 편지는 사람들을 설득할 만한 대단한 영향력을 가지고 있다.)
7. achieve → to achieve
→ (인내하는 것은 이 여행 중 성취하기 쉬운 것이 아니다.)

Exercise 1-1)
다음 문장을 문법에 맞게 고친 후 해석하세요.
1. do → to do
→ (그들은 오늘 밤 해야 할 숙제가 많다.)
2. eat → to eat
→ (난 배고프다. 나는 먹을 무엇인가가 필요하다.)
3. read → to read
→ (Jane은 읽을 얼마 간의 책을 샀다.)
4. visit → to visit
→ (서울은 방문할 좋은 장소이다.)
5. lose → to lose
→ (너는 잃을 것이 아무것도 없다.)
6. drive → to drive
→ (Andrew는 운전을 할 자동차를 구매했다.)
7. improve → to improve
→ (Harry는 그의 건강을 개선할 약들을 구매하였다.)

Exercise 2)
다음 괄호 안의 단어들을 적절히 배열하여 문장을 완성하세요.
1. I made a doll to give my daughter.
2. She doesn't have a pencil to write with .
3. Could you give me a chair to sit on?
4. I am so tired. I am looking for a bed to sleep in.
5. I have a lot of work to do.

Exercise 2-1)
다음 괄호 안의 단어들을 적절히 배열하여 문장을 완성하세요.
1. I have some pictures to show you.
2. I have no friend to play with.
3. He brought a baby to look after.
4. She is not a person to tell a lie.

Exercise 3)
다음 문장을 영작하세요. (예시답안입니다.)
1. I need something to eat.
2. I know someone to help her.
3. Can you give me a chair to sit on?
4. She doesn't have friends to play with.
5. He bought some magazines to read.

Exercise 3-1)
다음 문장을 영작하세요. (예시답안입니다.)
1. Would you like something to drink?
2. She is not a person to eat much like that.
3. I need someone to talk with.
4. Does Jack own a house to live in?
5. We have a lot of things to do.

Unit 20 to부정사의 부사적 용법
(1) 목적: ~하기 위해서
(2) 원인: ~하다니, ~해서
(3) 형용사 수식

Exercise 1)
다음 주어진 문장의 부사적 용법에 유의하며 해석하세요.
1. 그는 그의 친구를 만나기 위해 호주로 갈 것을 계획했다.
2. 그녀는 그에게 단지 작별 인사를 하기 위하여 전화했다.
3. 나는 너를 다시 보게 되어 정말로 행복하다.
4. 그는 그 영화를 보게 되어 너무 신난다.

5. 나는 사진을 찍기 위해 의자에 앉았다.

6. 우리는 어려움에 처한 사람들을 돕기 위해서 어떤 것이든 할 수 있다.

7. John은 홍수 피해자들을 돕기 위해서 천만 원을 기부했다.

8. 장기적인 계획을 세우는 것은 성공하는데 중요하다.

9. 나는 장학금을 받기 위해서 이 시험에 최선을 다할 것이다.

Exercise 1-1)

다음 주어진 문장의 부사적 용법에 유의하며 해석하세요.

1. 그 말을 듣게 되어 유감입니다.

2. 나는 평화를 기원하기 위해서 교회에 갔다.

3. 그녀는 사과하기 위해서 그에게 전화했다.

4. 나는 그 끔찍한 사건을 목격해서 충격 받았다.

5. 그 강은 수영하기에 위험하다.

6. Jane은 열심히 공부하기 위해서 도서관으로 가는 중이다.

7. Susan은 그녀의 어머니를 기쁘게 해드리기 위해서 집을 청소했다.

8. 우리는 베르사유 궁전을 방문하기 위해서 파리에 갈 것이다.

9. 그녀는 그룹으로 공부해서 행복하다.

Exercise 2)

다음 문장을 영작하세요. (예시답안입니다.)

1. I am glad to meet you.

2. She came to meet her mother.

3. We became sad to read the letter.

4. Her life is hard to understand.

5. He sat on the chair to write a letter.

Exercise 2-1)

다음 문장을 영작하세요. (예시답안입니다.)

1. I am running to catch the bus.

2. I just called to say thanks.

3. I went to the bank to borrow money.

4. He was moved to receive the envelope.

5. She was surprised to meet me by chance.

(4) too ~ to / enough to

Exercise 1) 다음 문장을 보기를 참고하여 바꾸세요.

1. He is too busy to call her.

2. She is too poor to buy a car.

3. John is kind enough to understand my son's rudeness.

4. Jane is too fat to wear the jeans.

5. I am tall enough to apply for a super model.

6. David is so selfish that he can't understand others' feelings.

7. They are brave enough to face the strong enemy.

8. The cat is too big to enter the room.

9. Bob got up too late to catch the bus.

10. She is too busy to spend time with her boyfriend.

Exercise 1-1) 다음 문장을 보기를 참고하여 바꾸세요.

1. He is too lazy to get up early in the morning.

2. He is kind enough to drive her home.

3. Jane is too weak to beat John.

4. She is beautiful enough to be famous at school.

5. I am too old to work anymore.

6. This problem is too difficult to solve.

7. We are too tired to go jogging now.

8. I am lucky enough to join your team.

9. This dog is too dirty to let him in.

10. She is too young to understand others' lives.

Exercise 2)

다음 문장을 영작하세요. (예시답안입니다.)

1. I am too young to swim.

2. I am tall enough to play basketball well.

3. He is strong enough to beat me.

4. She is too lazy to get up early.

5. John is healthy enough to swim.

6. He got up early enough to get on the train.

7. He was too poor to pay the rent.

8. Brian is smart enough to understand the problem.

9. He is influential enough to change the law.

Exercise 2-1)

다음 문장을 영작하세요. (예시답안입니다.)

1. She is too sleepy to read the book.
2. He is fast enough to catch up with a bus.
3. He is too poor to buy the house.
4. The dog is too dirty to let in this(the) building.
5. She is kind enough to help her friend.
6. The used car is good enough to give to my younger brother(sister).
7. He is too fat to wear the shirt.
8. She is fast enough to arrive on time.
9. Julie is too weak to move this desk.

Exercise 2-1)

다음 문장을 영작하세요. (예시답안입니다.)

1. It is not difficult for me to make you smile.
2. I pretended not to know the fact.
3. I have a great way for them to understand it.
4. I tried not to cry.
5. This bicycle is not easy for Jane to ride.

■ **단원별 문제** -본문 151 페이지
┃ **Chapter 5 to 부정사**
┃   **Unit 17-21**

Unit 21 부정형 및 의미상 주어

(1) 부정형

(2) 의미상의 주어

Exercise 1) **다음 문장을 해석하세요.**

1. 그녀가 가난한 사람들을 무시한 것은 현명하지 않았다.
2. 정부는 모든 마을 사람들이 환경을 보존하도록 정책을 폈다.
3. 나는 네가 프랑스어 문법을 이해할 대단한 방법을 가지고 있다.
4. 우리가 아무 말도 하지 않은 것은 영리했다.
5. 나는 누군가를 기다리는 것이 어렵다.

Exercise 2)

다음 문장을 영작하세요. (예시답안입니다.)

1. It is easy for me to solve the problem.
2. It is difficult for John to make fire.
3. I decided not to talk with him.
4. It is important for me to pass the exam.
5. It is not hard for him to run fast.

1. 명사적 용법_주어
tip! 이 문장은 진주어, 가주어 구문이다.
그 문제를 분명하게 이해하는 것은 어려웠다.
2. 부사적 용법
그녀를 만족시키기 위해서, 나는 자주 미소짓기 시작했다.
3. 형용사적 용법
나는 점심으로 먹을 약간의 샐러드를 만들었다.
4. 명사적 용법_목적어
나의 어머니는 정말로 나를 돕길 원했다.
5. ①
tip!
보기에 사용된 to부정사는 명사적 용법 중에서도 보어로 사용된 것이다.
② 부사적 용법 '~하기 위해서'
③ 부사적 용법: 감정단어와 함께
④ 형용사적 용법: a lot of novels 수식
⑤ 형용사적 용법: friends 수식
6. ②
tip!
②번에 쓰인 to부정사는 '~하기 위해서'로 해석되는 부사적 용법인 반면 나머지는 전부 앞에 있는 명사를 수식하는 형용사적 용법으로 사용됐다.
7. ④
tip!
모두 명사적 용법으로 쓰이긴 했으나 그 중에서도

④은 보어의 역할을 하고 있고 나머지는 주어 역할을 하고 있다.
8. ④
tip!
④은 형용사적 용법으로 쓰였으며 나머지는 명사적 용법이다.
9. ③
10. ①, ⑤
tip!
too~to: 너무~해서 ~할 수 없다
11. ①
② how should ride a bicycle → how they should ride a bicycle 또는 how to ride a bicycle
③ to write → to write with
④ want play → want to play
⑤ difficult learn → difficult to learn
12. ①
tip!
② to play → to play with
③ to live → to live in
④ to write → to write on
⑤ to sell to → to sell
13. 목적어
14. 보어
15. 주어
16. ①
tip!
①은 of가 들어가고 나머지는 for이 들어간다.
17. ②
tip!
②은 명사적 용법 중에서도 want의 목적어 역할을 하고 있으며 나머지는 앞에 있는 명사를 꾸며주는 형용사적 용법으로 쓰였다.
18. ③
19. ④
tip!
ⓐ 부사적 용법 (좋은 친구를 사귀기 위해서, 우선 좋은 사람이 되라.)
ⓑ 명사적 용법_목적어 (나는 내년에 경제학을 전공하려 의도한다.)

ⓒ 형용사적 용법 (나는 가지고 쓸 펜을 사야한다.)
ⓓ 형용사적 용법 (그녀는 나를 도와줄 바로 첫 번째 사람이다.)
ⓔ 명사적 용법_보어 (나의 아버지의 꿈은 파일럿이 되는 것이었다.)
20. to wear
21. to buy
22. ④
23. what to do
24. ④
25. (1) to buy, to live in
    (2) a chair to sit on

Chapter 6 동명사와 분사

Unit 22 동명사의 명사적 역할
Exercise 1)
다음 밑줄 친 동명사의 역할을 쓰세요. (주어/보어/목적어)
1. 주어 (기타를 연주하는 것은 재밌다.)
2. 목적어 (우리는 수영하는 것을 즐긴다.)
3. 보어 (나의 취미는 낮잠 자는 것이다.)
4. 목적어 (언제 너는 담배를 끊었니?)
5. 보어 (나의 계획은 전 세계를 여행하는 것이다.)
6. 목적어 (그녀는 그것을 하려고 시도했다.)
7. 목적어 (나는 당신을 만났던 것을 기억한다.)
8. 주어 (그 음악을 듣는 것은 내가 일상의 스트레스를 줄이는데 도움을 준다.

Exercise 1-1)
다음 밑줄 친 동명사의 역할을 쓰세요. (주어/보어/목적어)
1. 주어 (깜짝 파티를 준비하는 것이 나의 임무다.)
2. 목적어 (오늘 아침 비가 오기 시작했다.)
3. 목적어 (창문을 열면 싫겠니?)
4. 주어 (혼자 사는 것이 속 편하다.)
5. 주어 (수영하는 것이 네가 살아있음을 느끼게 해준다.)
6. 보어 (나의 계획은 큰 집을 사는 것이다.)
7. 주어 (지역 음식을 먹는 것이 나의 여행의 묘미이다.)
8. 보어 (중요한 것은 최선을 다하는 것이다.)

Exercise 2)
다음 문장을 동명사를 활용하여 영작하세요.
(예시답안입니다.)
1. The important thing in your life is loving people.
2. Understanding other people is not easy.
3. I enjoy drinking at the bar.
4. Talking with people is my happiness.
5. He quit bothering her.

Unit 23 동명사와 to부정사
(1) 주어
(2) 보어
(3) 목적어

Exercise 1) **다음 문장 중 틀린 부분을 고치세요.**
1. will be → to be /being
2. studying → to study
3. To speaking → To speak /Speaking
4. to open → opening
5. to read → reading
6. being → to be
7. to crying → to cry /crying
8. meeting → to meet
9. to say → saying
10. meeting → to meet

Exercise 2)
다음 주어진 문장을 to부정사 또는 동명사를 활용해서 영작하세요. (예시답안입니다.)
1. He wants to play basketball.
2. She learned to write in English.
3. The important thing is to love friends.
4. To be with you is my pleasure. (=Being with you is my pleasure.)
5. I told him to close the door.
6. To see is to believe. (=Seeing is believing.)
7. My hobby is to paint(=painting).
8. I gave up painting him.
9. I wish to see you again.
10. I want you to come back home.

Exercise 2-1)
다음 주어진 문장을 to부정사 또는 동명사를 활용해서 영작하세요. (예시답안입니다.)
1. We decided to go shopping.
2. I want to be a dentist.
3. I stopped to smoke.

본편 157 페이지

4. I stopped smoking.

5. He promised to stop smoking.

6. We stopped fighting.

7. They stopped to fight.

8. You forgot meeting her.

9. You should remember to meet her tomorrow.

10. He denied stealing the book.

Unit 24 분사의 형용사적 용법

(1) 현재분사

(2) 과거분사

Exercise 1) 다음 괄호 안에 적절한 형태에 O표 하세요.

1. dancing (춤추고 있는 소녀들이 천사처럼 보인다.)

2. used (나는 돈 문제 때문에 중고 자전거를 샀다.)

3. written (나는 영어로 쓰인 소설책 한 권을 읽었다.)

4. sleeping (우리는 화장실에서 자고 있는 아기를 봤다.)

5. exciting (이 컴퓨터 게임은 무척 흥미진진하다.)

6. built (여기에 세워진 빌딩은 그에게 팔릴 것이다.)

7. cooked (그에 의해서 요리된 그 고기가 아직도 제공되지 않았다.)

8. touching, moved (그 영화는 매우 감동적이었다, 그래서 나는 매우 감동받았다.)

9. surprised, surprising (그는 그 놀라운 결과에 의해 놀랐다.)

Exercise 1-1) 다음 괄호 안에 적절한 형태에 O표 하세요.

1. crying, broken (부서진 집에 몇몇의 울고 있는 아기들이 있다.)

2. named (나는 어제 Sally라고 이름 지어진 소녀를 만났다.)

3. sleeping (나무 아래서 자고 있는 남자를 봐.)

4. flying (그들은 하늘을 날고 있는 그 새를 쐈다.)

5. broken (당신은 언제 그 부서진 문을 고칠 것입니까?)

6. Used, recycling (사용된 종이와 캔들은 재활용통

에 놓여야만 한다.)

7. unexpected (당신은 예기치 못한 위험에 직면할지도 모른다.)

8. boiled (나는 끓여진 달걀(삶은 달걀)을 먹는 것에 질린다.)

9. cooking (나는 Jane이 부엌에서 요리하고 있는 것을 봤다.

10. caught (나는 강에서 고래가 잡히는 것을 본적이 없다.)

■ **단원별 문제** -본문 169 페이지

| **Chapter 6 동명사와 분사**
| **Unit 22-24**

1. ④

2. ⑤

tip!

전치사 뒤에는 명사나 명사의 역할을 하는 동명사가 올 수있다.

3. ①

tip!

① mind + ing: 꺼리다

② stop+ing: ~하는 것을 멈추다

③ enjoy+ing: ~하는 것을 즐기다

4. ②

tip!

② put off는 동명사를 받는 동사이다.

put off, delay, postpone + ing (미루다)

5. ③

tip!

해석: 최근에 출판된 많은 영어 사전에서, 우리는 많은 새로운 단어를 발견할 수 있다.

6. yelling

tip!

해석: 그녀에게 소리치고 있는 소년은 그녀의 남자형제이다.

7. named

tip!
해석: 민지라고 이름 지어진 그 소녀는 매우 예쁘다.
8. to pay
tip!
해석: 그는 한 달 내에 돈을 돌려준다고 약속했다.
9. to help
tip!
해석: Harry는 친절히 내가 좋은 의사를 찾도록 돕는데 동의했다.
10. to see
tip!
해석: 나는 그녀를 다시 보리라고 결코 기대하지 않았다.
11. ④
tip!
④에서 want는 to부정사와 함께 쓰는 동사이다.
12. ②
tip!
②번은 be동사와 함께 현재진행시제로 쓰인 것이고 나머지는 명사적 용법으로 보어자리에 놓인 것이다. 따라서 ②번을 제외한 나머지는 용법이 중복되는 to부정사와 바꿔 써도 무방하다.
13. ①
tip!
①번에 쓰인 running은 현재분사이다. 분사는 형용사역할을 하기 때문에 여기서는 뒤에 있는 dog를 꾸며준다. ①번을 제외한 나머지는 모두 동명사로 쓰였다.
14. ①
tip!
① barked → barking
능동적으로 '짖고 있는'것이므로 barking이 적절하다.
② refused by her이 the boy 수식 (그녀에 의해 거절당한 그 소년은 외출을 원하지 않았다.)
③ 전치사 다음에 동명사 사용
④ lying on the couch가 the man 수식 (소파에 누워있는 그 남자는 막 잠들 것 같다.)
⑤ smiling이 girl 수식 (그 미소 짓고 있는 소녀는 매력적으로 보인다.)

15. slept → sleeping
16. ④
17. to drink
18. ⑤
tip!
to swim → swimming
19. ③
tip!
to help → help: 문장에 본동사가 없다
20. ⑤
tip!
전치사 뒤에는 명사나 동명사만 올 수 있다.
21. ②
tip!
②에 쓴 to 부정사는 부사적 용법으로 쓰였다.
22. ①
tip!
① Meet → Meeting(To meet)
주어가 없는 문장이므로 동사에 ing 또는 to부정사를 붙여 주어역할을 할 수 있는 준동사로 활용한다.
23. to solve /solving, reading
24. ⑤
tip!
be busy ~ing: ~하느라 바쁘다
25. Start → To start 또는 Starting~

Chapter 7 등위접속사

Unit 25 등위접속사와 병렬
Exercise 1)
다음 괄호 안에 적절한 접속사를 써 넣으세요.
1. for
2. and
3. but
4. or
5. so
6. or
7. so
8. but

Exercise 1-1)
다음 괄호 안에 적절한 접속사를 써 넣으세요.
1. so
2. but
3. so
4. or
5. but
6. but
7. but
8. for

Exercise 2) 다음 문장을 해석하세요.
1. 우리는 돈을 저축하고 그 집을 사기로 결정했다.
2. 그들은 맥주를 마시고 서로 수다 떠는 것을 즐긴다.
3. 사랑하는 것과 사랑 받는 것은 삶에서 가장 위대한 행복이다.
4. 언어는 모든 지식과 모든 힘의 근본이다.
5. 모든 것을 하는 것 혹은 모든 것을 가지는 것은 가능하지 않다.
6. 제게 시원한 무엇인가, 맛있는 무엇인가 그리고 비싼 무엇인가를 주실 수 있나요?

Exercise 2-1) 다음 문장을 해석하세요.
1. 사는 것과 빌리는 것 중 무엇이 나을까?
2. 많은 우유를 마시고, 규칙적으로 운동을 하는 것이 어때?
3. 일찍 일어나는 것은 너를 상쾌하게 만들고 너에게 건강한 삶을 제공한다.
4. 나의 목표는 너그러워 지는 것과, 야망이 있어 지는 것과, 부자가 되는 것이다.
5. 그들은 쌀로 만든 새 상품들을 개발했고, 그 상품들을 합리적인 가격에 팔았다.

Exercise 3)
다음 문장을 and/or/but을 이용하여 영작하세요.
(예시답안 입니다.)
1. My mother bought me a house and a car.
2. Which do you prefer between summer and winter?
3. I went to the library and studied history.
4. She is pretty but bad-tempered.
5. You are kidding or crazy.

Exercise 3-1)
다음 문장을 and/or/but을 이용하여 영작하세요.
(예시답안 입니다.)
1. My mother bought me some bread and milk.
2. He likes swimming but hates the sea.
3. You can take a bus or a taxi.
4. He studied hard and got good grade in the final test.
5. Tom is living in Itaewon and working around there.

Unit 26 등위상관접속사와 병렬
Exercise 1) 다음 문장을 보기와 같이 고치세요.
1. He has money problems as well as health problems.
2. Tom as well as Jane can swim well.
3. Tom bought her a house as well as a car.
4. LQ as well as Samsung is in debt.
5. We play baseball as well as soccer together.

본문 175 페이지

Exercise 1-1) 다음 문장을 보기와 같이 고치세요.
1. Not only her dog but also Sally came back to the house.
2. I want to not only read this book but also own it.
3. This rule applies
① to not only children but also parents.
② not only to children but also to parents.
4. We are eating not only noodles but also rice.
5. She is not only brave but also beautiful.

Exercise 2) 다음 문장을 영작하세요. (2가지)
1.
→ He is not only brave but also honest.
→ He is honest as well as brave.
2.
→ Not only my friends but also I am good at swimming.
→ I as well as my friends am good at swimming.
3.
→ They like not only meat but also fish.
→ They like fish as well as meat.
4.
→ She is not only beautiful but also rich.
→ She is rich as well as beautiful.
5.
→ This product is the best not only in price but also in quality.
→ This product is the best in quality as well as in price.

Exercise 2-1) 다음 문장을 영작하세요. (2가지)
1.
→ He is not only tall but also handsome.
→ He is handsome as well as tall.
2.
→ John likes not only listening to music but also singing.
→ John likes singing as well as listening to music.
3.
→ Not only they but also I was invited to the party.

→ I as well as they was invited to the party.
4.
→ It(This) can be not only bought but also sold.
→ It(This) can be sold as well as bought.
5.
→ I like not only a watermelon but also an orange.
→ I like an orange as well as a watermelon.

■ 단원별 문제 -본문 185 페이지
Chapter 7. 등위접속사
unit 25-26

1. ②
2. ②
3. ④
tip!
or → and
4. ③
5. ④
6. ③
7. ⑤
tip!
or → and
8. but also
9. ②
10. ③
11. ③
tip!
both A and B: A, B 둘 다
12. ②
13. ④
tip!
④은 and가 들어가고 나머지는 or을 넣어야 적절하다.
14. ③
tip!
are → is

15. ⑤
16. ④
17. ②
tip!
or → nor
18. ②

Unit 27 명사절을 이끄는 접속사

(1) that과 what
Exercise 1)
주어진 두 개의 접속사 중에서 올바른 것을 고르세요.

(주어)
1. That (그가 새로운 여자 친구를 사귀었다는 것이 나를 질투하게 만들었다.)
2. What (그녀를 괴롭히는 것은 파리이다.)

(보어)
1. that (나의 바람들 중에 하나는 세계에 전쟁이 없게 되는 것이다.
2. what (그 대답은 그녀가 결정한 것이다.)

(목적어)
1. that (나는 우리가 그들의 도움을 필요로 한다는 것을 나타냈다.)
2. what (나는 그녀가 진짜 가지길 원했던 것을 사주었다.)

(2) if /whether
Exercise 1-1)
주어진 두 개의 접속사 중에서 올바른 것을 고르세요.

(주어)
1. That (내가 수학시험에서 C를 받았다는 것이 놀랍지 않다.)
2. Whether (그녀가 그것을 좋아할지 안할지가 나에게 불분명하다.)

(보어)
1. that (이 팀의 목표는 그 구역이 깨끗해지는 것이다.)
2. what (그 상품의 좋은 품질은 그 고객을 만족시켰던 것이다.)

(목적어)
1. whether (나는 그의 증언이 진실된 지 아닌지 모르겠다.)
2. that (제발, 나에게 당신이 그냥 괜찮다고 말해주세요.)

(3) 의문사절

Exercise 1-2)

주어진 두 개의 접속사 중에서 올바른 것을 고르세요.

(주어)

1. When (언제 내가 그를 만났는지가 그들에게 중요하다.)
2. How (얼마나 오래 내가 그를 만나왔는지가 그들에게 중요하다.)

(보어)

1. how (핵심은 그것이 얼마나 많이 값이 나갈 것이냐에 있다.)
2. when (그의 질문은 인수가 언제 그녀를 만났냐는 것이다.)

(목적어)

1. whose (나는 그에게 이것이 누구의 책인지를 말했다.)
2. what (나의 표정이 내가 정말로 원하는 것을 보여줬다.)

Exercise 1-3)

주어진 두 개의 접속사 중에서 올바른 것을 고르세요.

(주어)

1. Who (누가 대통령이 될 지는 우리의 선택에 달려있다.)
2. Which (어떤 색을 그가 선택하는 지가 규칙을 바꿀 수 있다.)

(보어)

1. where (문제는 그가 어디서 사느냐이다.)
2. which (그 결과는 그들이 어떤 옵션을 클릭하는지에 달려있다.)

(목적어)

1. why (나의 딸은 왜 하늘이 파란지를 궁금해 하고 있다.)
2. how (나는 그가 어떻게 수학에 흥미가 생겼는지 안다.)

▶ 단원 결합문제 (Unit 27) -본문 196 페이지

Exercise 1)

괄호 안에 알맞은 표현을 고르고 해석하세요.

1. what (그는 나에게 내가 그로부터 듣고 싶어 하는 것을 결코 말해주지 않는다.)
2. Whether (그녀가 한국어를 할 수 있는지 없는지가 불확실하다.)
3. Whether (당신의 아버지가 부유한지 아닌지는 중요하지 않다.)
4. why (나는 왜 그가 수영을 잘할 수 있는지 궁금하다.)
5. what (이것이 그가 가지길 원하는 것이다.)
6. that (그녀는 내가 거짓말쟁이라는 것을 믿지 않는다.)
7. that (나는 이것이 숟가락이라고 생각한다.)
8. How (내가 어떻게 나의 삶을 살아왔는지가 그의 선택에 영향을 미칠 수 있다.)
9. what (그것이 바로 내가 하도록 의미한 것이다.)
10. whether (당신이 파티에 참여할 수 있는지 아닌지 알려주세요.)

Exercise 2)

다음 밑줄 친 명사절이 문장에서 어떤 역할을 하는지 쓰고 해석하세요.

1. 보어 (문제는 왜 그가 그렇게 말했냐는 것이다.)
2. 목적어 (나는 내가 날 수 있다고 믿는다.)
3. 주어 (네가 수영을 할 수 있는지 없는지는 문제가 아니다.)
4. 목적어 (나는 그녀가 제 시간에 돌아올 지 궁금하다.)
5. 보어 (문제는 내가 차가 없다는 것이다.)

Exercise 2-1)

다음 밑줄 친 명사절이 문장에서 어떤 역할을 하는지 쓰고 해석하세요.

1. 목적어 (네가 준비됐는지 알게 해줘.)
2. 주어 (그가 그녀를 사랑하는 지가 불확실하다.)
3. 목적어 (나는 이것이 사과라고 생각한다.)
4. 주어 (그가 정직한지가 불확실하다.)
5. 보어 (그의 꿈은 그가 세계의 평화를 위해 무언가를 할 수 있게 되는 것이다.)

Exercise 3)

다음 문장을 적절한 접속사를 써서 영작하세요.
(예시답안입니다.)

1. My opinion is that I object to the rule.
2. I don't know what you want to have.
3. That you will become 20 (years old) soon is surprising. (=It is surprising that you will become 20 (years old) soon.)
4. Can you guess what they are talking about?
5. I can't remember whether I have met her before.

Exercise 3-1)

다음 문장을 적절한 접속사를 써서 영작하세요.
(예시답안입니다.)

1. I guess that he is kind.
2. That she is good at English is certain.
(= It is certain that she is good at English.)
3. I wish that your dream comes true.
4. The problem is that we don't know each other.
5. That she is a criminal is shocking. (=It is shocking that she is a criminal.)

(4) 간접의문문
Exercise 1)

다음 두 문장을 합쳐서 하나의 간접의문문으로 만드세요.

1. Do you know why she was angry?
2. I don't know when the school begins.
3. I am not sure where the restroom is.
4. I don't remember what her e-mail address was.
5. I wonder what time it is now.

Exercise 1-1)

다음 두 문장을 합쳐서 하나의 간접의문문으로 만드세요.

1. I want to know whether she will come back.
2. Please tell me which car you like better.
3. Do you know how old she is?
4. She asked me how much the bag is.
5. I wonder whether it will rain tonight.

Unit 28 형용사절을 이끄는 접속사 (관계대명사)

(1) 관계대명사의 종류

(2) 관계대명사의 생략

Exercise 1)

다음 주어진 문장을 분석하고 해석하세요.

1. I was impressed by a girl (who delivered a speech.) (나는 연설을 하는 소녀를 보고 감명 받았다.)
2. The dog (that barks every day) is annoying. (매일 짖는 그 개는 성가시다.)
3. The scientist explained the substance (which he found). (그 과학자는 그가 발견한 물질에 대해 설명했다.
4. The girl (who hid her real intention) has bothered me. (그녀의 진짜 의도를 숨긴 소녀는 나를 괴롭혀왔다.)
5. He expects a miracle (that will make him pass the exam). (그는 시험을 통과시켜 줄 기적을 기대한다.)

Exercise 1-1)

다음 주어진 문장을 분석하고 해석하세요.

1. I have a watch (which I found on the street). (나는 길에서 발견한 손목시계를 갖고 있다.)
2. They got the snake (which bit him). (그들은 그를 문 뱀을 잡았다.)
3. He relies on a woman (who gave him a lot of money). 그는 그에게 많은 돈을 준 한 여자한테 의지한다.
4. We are looking for a vet (who can cure my dog). (우리는 나의 개를 치료할 수 있는 수의사를 찾고 있다
5. Anyone (who likes to run) can join this club. (달리기를 좋아하는 사람 누구나 이 클럽에 가입할 수 있다.)

Exercise 2)

다음 괄호 안에 that을 제외한 적절한 관계대명사를 써 넣으세요.

1. who
2. who
3. whose
4. which
5. whose
6. which
7. who(m)
8. which
9. who
10. which

Exercise 2-1)

다음 괄호 안에 that을 제외한 적절한 관계대명사를 써 넣으세요.

1. who(m)
2. who
3. whose
4. which
5. whose
6. which
7. which
8. which
9. which
10. whose

Unit 29 부사절을 이끄는 접속사

(1) 시간과 조건의 부사절

(2) 양보의 부사절

(3) 조건의 부사절

(4) 양보의 부사절

(5) 결과의 부사절

Exercise 1)

다음 괄호 안에서 적절한 표현을 고르세요.

1. If
2. when
3. While
4. when
5. When
6. Although
7. Although
8. Until
9. that
10. when

Exercise 1-1)

다음 빈칸에 적절한 부사절을 이끄는 접속사를 쓰세요.

1. when
2. Although
3. that
4. Unless
5. Before
6. When
7. When
8. that
9. because
10. Unless

Exercise 2)

다음 문장을 주어진 단어를 활용하여 영작하세요.

1. He is so fat that he can't run fast.
2. If the weather permits, we'll go on a picnic.
3. Although /Though /Even though she is young, she expresses her opinion well.
4. Tom had so many things to do that he didn't have lunch.
5. Although /Though /Even though he is old enough, he still likes reading comic books.

Exercise 2-1)

다음 주어진 문장을 영작하세요. (예시답안입니다.)

1. The problem is so difficult that anyone can't solve it.
2. If we don't hurry, we will miss the bus.
3. If you meet him, he will confess his guilt.
4. He is so tall that he can be a basketball player.
5. He has so much money that he can buy the house.
6. If you don't take a nap now, you will be so tired tonight.

■ **단원별 문제** -본문 213 페이지
| **Chapter 8. 종속접속사**
|　　unit 27-29

1. because
2. while
3. since
4. ③
5. ①
6. ④
tip!
Jina는 학생이기 때문에, 그녀는 공부를 열심히 해야 한다.
7. ⑤
8. ④
tip!
after 대신에 because 정도가 괜찮다.
9. ⑤
tip!
happens → happened
10. ④

tip!
Poly는 친구를 쉽게 사귄다, 왜냐하면 그녀가 외향적이기 때문에.

11. ①
tip!
비록 그가 돈에 대해 관대할지라도, 그는 그의 돈을 낭비하지는 않는다.
12. ④
tip!
그가 학급으로 돌아왔을 때, 그는 파티에 놀랐다.
13. ②
tip!
내가 그 소녀를 좋아하기 때문에, 나는 그녀의 눈도 마주칠 수가 없다.
2015년 이래로, 나는 그 콘서트를 참석해오고 있다.
14. ③
15. ④
tip!
소미가 매우 어릴지라도, 그녀는 이 기사를 이해할 수 있다.
16. ②
tip!
시간과 조건의 부사절에서는 현재시제가 미래시제를 대신한다.
17. ⑤
tip!
won't rain → doesn't rain
18. ⑤
19. Don't eat anything until your father starts eating.
20. ②, ⑤
tip!
그 아이들은 실망했다 왜냐하면 그들이 그 영웅을 만나도록 선택되지 않았기 때문에.
21. ④
tip!
will give → give
22. ⑤
tip!
내가 여전히 교실에 있기 때문에, 그들은 나를 밖에서 기다려야만 한다.

23. ②
tip!
보상이 대단하기 때문에 너는 포기하지 않는 것
이 낫겠다.
24. ④
25. it rains

Chapter 9 대명사

Unit 30 인칭대명사
Exercise 1) 다음 인칭대명사표의 빈칸을 채우세요.

주격	소유격	목적격	소유대명사	재귀대명사
I	my	me	mine	myself
we	our	us	ours	ourselves
you	your	you	yours	yourself
you	your	you	yours	yourselves
he	his	him	his	himself
she	her	her	hers	herself
it	its	it		itself
they	their	them	theirs	themselves

Exercise 1-1) 다음 인칭대명사표의 빈칸을 채우세요.

주격	소유격	목적격	소유대명사	재귀대명사
I	my	me	mine	myself
we	our	us	ours	ourselves
you	your	you	yours	yourself
you	your	you	yours	yourselves
he	his	him	his	himself
she	her	her	hers	herself
it	its	it		itself
they	their	them	theirs	themselves

Exercise 2) 다음 밑줄 친 부분을 한 단어로 쓰세요.
1. mine
2. hers
3. theirs
4. his
5. yours
6. ours

Exercise 2-1) 다음 밑줄 친 부분을 한 단어로 쓰세요.

1. yours
2. theirs
3. mine
4. his
5. ours
6. hers

Exercise 3) 다음 중 옳은 형태를 고르세요.

1. mine
2. You
3. his
4. himself
5. yours
6. yourself
7. myself

Exercise 3-1) 다음 중 옳은 형태를 고르세요.

1. me
2. them
3. ourselves
4. his
5. myself
6. herself
7. him
8. himself

Exercise 4) 우리말에 맞게 빈칸을 채우세요.

1. yours
2. My
3. yourself
4. They, themselves
5. myself
6. itself
7. Their
8. me
9. themselves

Exercise 4-1) 우리말에 맞게 빈칸을 채우세요.

1. mine
2. themselves
3. his
4. You
5. herself
6. itself
7. Our
8. Mine, his
9. yourself

Unit 31 비인칭 it

Exercise 1) 다음 문장을 it을 활용하여 영작하세요.

1. It is raining now.
2. How far is it from Seoul to Daejun?
3. What time is it now?
4. It is sunny today.

Exercise 1-1) 다음 문장을 it을 활용하여 영작하세요.

1. It is summer now.
2. It's 8:30 p.m. now.
3. It's cold today.
4. How far is it from here to your house?

Unit 32 부정대명사 1

(1) some /any

Exercise 1)

다음 문장에서 some과 any 중 더 적절한 것을 고르세요.

1. something
2. some
3. any
4. some
5. any
6. Some

Exercise 1-1)
다음 문장에서 some과 any 중 더 적절한 것을 고르세요.
1. some
2. any
3. any
4. some
5. some
6. any

Exercise 2)
다음 문장에서 some과 any 중 더 적절한 것을 적으세요.
1. some
2. any
3. Some
4. any
5. any
6. any

Exercise 2-1)
다음 문장에서 some과 any 중 더 적절한 것을 적으세요.
1. some
2. any
3. Some
4. any
5. some
6. any

(2) all /both
Exercise 1)
다음 문장 속 all과 both의 용법으로 옳은 것을 고르고 해석하세요.
1. 형용사 (나는 모든 사람들이 동등하다고 믿는다.)
2. 전치한정사 (모든 식물들은 빛과 물을 필요로 한다.)
3. 대명사 (형제 둘 다 매우 똑똑하다.)
4. 형용사 (두 학생 모두 숙제를 하지 않았다.)
5. 대명사 (모두가 행복하지 않다.)

Exercise 1-1)
다음 문장 속 all과 both의 용법으로 옳은 것을 고르고 해석하세요.
1. 대명사 (우리 둘 다 최선을 다했다.)
2. 전치한정사 (모든 학생들은 보고서를 제출해야 한다.)
3. 형용사 (모든 개들은 사랑스럽다.)
4. 대명사 (그들은 매우 달라보이지만, 둘 다 괜찮다.)
5. 전치한정사 (두 선생님 모두 학생들에게 너무 엄격하다.)

Exercise 2)
All과 Both를 활용하여 다음 빈칸을 채우세요.
1. All, the, seats
2. both
3. Both
4. Both, of, us
5. All, the, leaves

Exercise 2-1)
All과 Both를 활용하여 다음 빈칸을 채우세요.
1. All, his, money
2. Both
3. both
4. All, the, boys
5. both, you.

(3) each /every
Excercise 1)
다음 문장의 밑줄 친 부분을 바르게 고쳐 쓰세요.
1. ships → ship
2. student → students
3. each → every
4. have → has
5. classes → class
6. hate → hates
7. minute → minutes
8. words → word

Excercise 1-1)

빈칸에 적절한 단어를 보기에서 골라 채워 넣으세요.

(둘 다 가능할 수 있음)

1. Each

2. Each/Every

3. Each

4. each

5. every

6. Each/Every

7. Each/Every

8. Each

9. Each/Every

Exercise 2) 다음 문장의 빈칸을 채우세요.

1. Every, person, has

2. each

3. Every, human being, is

4. Each, has

5. Every, student, studies

Exercise 2-1) 다음 문장의 빈칸을 채우세요.

1. Each, question, gives

2. every, student,

3. every, minute

4. every, article

5. Each, us

Unit 33 부정대명사 2

(1) It과 one

Exercise 1)

빈칸에 적절한 단어를 보기에서 골라 채워 넣으세요.

1. one

2. it

3. one

4. ones

5. them, it

6. ones

7. one

8. them

9. it

10. it

Exercise 1-1)

빈칸에 적절한 단어를 보기에서 골라 채워 넣으세요.

1. ones

2. one

3. it

4. them

5. them

6. ones

7. one

8. them

9. one

10. it

Exercise 1-2)

빈칸에 적절한 단어를 보기에서 골라 채워 넣으세요.

1. ones

2. it

3. one

4. it

5. them

6. ones

7. them

8. one

9. ones

10. them

(2) one~, the other...:

(3) one~, the others...:

(4) one~, another..., the other-:

(5) ① some~, others...:

　　② some~, the others...:

Exercise 1)

빈칸에 적절한 단어를 보기에서 골라 채워 넣으세요.
1. others
2. the other
3. another
4. the others
5. another, the other
6. others
7. The others
8. another
9. the others
10. the other

Exercise 1-1)

빈칸에 적절한 단어를 보기에서 골라 채워 넣으세요.
1. the other
2. the others
3. others
4. another, the other
5. the other
6. the others
7. another
8. the other
9. others
10. the others

Excercise 1-2)

빈칸에 적절한 단어를 보기에서 골라 채워 넣으세요.
1. One, the other
2. One, another, the other
3. The others
4. some, others

5. Some, the others
6. One, the other
7. One, another, the other
8. One, the others
9. another
10. the others

■ 단원별 문제　-본문 246 페이지

Chapter 9. 대명사
　unit 30-32

1. ④
2. of itself
3. ③
4. ③
5. another
6. ④
7. ②
8. ④
tip!
Between ourselves: 우리끼리 이야기지만
9. ⑤
tip!
⑤은 가짜주어 it인데 나머지는 모두 비인칭 주어로 쓰인 it이다.
10. ④
11. ①
12. 장난감 칼
13. Between ourselves
14. his
15. himself
16. Ours
17. ①
tip!
보기 중에 복수 취급하는 것은 both 밖에 없다.
18. ⑤
19. ②

Chapter 10 비교급

Unit 34 비교

(1) 비교급과 최상급 만들기

Exercise 1)

다음 주어진 단어의 비교급과 최상급을 만드세요.

1. healthy → healthier, healthiest
2. cool → cooler, coolest
3. strong → stronger, strongest
4. many/much → more, most
5. few → fewer, fewest
6. small → smaller, smallest
7. weak → weaker, weakest
8. late → later, latest
9. rough → rougher, roughest
10. helpful → more helpful, most helpful

Exercise 1-1)

다음 주어진 단어의 비교급과 최상급을 만드세요.

1. young → younger, youngest
2. hard → harder, hardest
3. cold → colder, coldest
4. stylish → more stylish, most stylish
5. cute → cuter, cutest
6. hungry → hungrier, hungriest
7. wise → wiser, wisest
8. difficult → more difficult, most difficult
9. interesting → more interesting, most interesting
10. old → older, oldest

(2) 원급 비교

(3) 비교

(4) 비교급 강조 수식어

Exercise 1) 다음 문장을 문법에 맞게 고치세요.

1. tall → taller
2. more strong → stronger
3. wide → wider
4. more big → bigger
5. prettyer → prettier

---

tip!
보기에 사용된 it은 비인칭 주어 it이다.

20. ②
21. ②
22. ①
23. ③

tip!
동사가 enjoy로 복수형이라서 both가 적절하다.

24. ⑤
25. ④

본문 252 페이지

Exercise 1-1)

다음 문장을 문법에 맞게 고치세요.

1. oldest → older
2. expensiver → more expensive
3. beautiful she → beautiful than she
4. tall → taller
5. more clean → cleaner

Exercise 1-2)

다음 문장을 문법에 맞게 고치세요.

1. stronger → strong
2. very → much/far/still/a lot/even
3. heavy the cat → heavy as the cat
4. a lot of → much/far/still/a lot/even
5. many → much/far/still/a lot/even

Unit 35 최상급

(1) 최상급의 구성
(2) 비교급으로 최상급 표현하기

Exercise 1)

두 문장이 같은 의미가 되도록 빈칸을 채우세요.

1. the, highest
2. more, than
3. the, most
4. smarter
5. larger, than
6. the, biggest, No, bigger

Exercise 1-1)

두 문장이 같은 의미가 되도록 빈칸을 채우세요.

1. the, prettiest
2. No, more, than
3. more, than
4. stronger, than
5. the, most, delicious

Exercise 2) 다음 주어진 문장의 빈칸을 채우세요.

1. sweeter, than
2. more, important, than
3. far, prettier, than
4. the, tallest, boy
5. more, spectacular, than
6. faster, than
7. three, years, older, than

Exercise 2-1) 다음 주어진 문장의 빈칸을 채우세요.

1. one, the fastest
2. the biggest
3. the, most, important
4. not, cool, as
5. the most, expensive
6. the, best, singer
7. as, smart, as

■ 단원별 문제 -본문 263 페이지
Chapter 10. 비교급
    unit 34-35

1. ②
tip!
big-bigger-biggest
2. ⑤
tip!
little-less-least
3. ⑤
4. as strong as
5. ③
tip!
as heavier as → as heavy as
6. ①, ③
tip!
일반 부사로는 비교급을 강조하지 않는다.

맨 255 페이지

7. ③

8. ①

tip!

hard의 비교급에는 more이 붙지 않고 harder이다.

9. ①

10. ⑤

11. ④, ⑤

tip!

more ugly → uglier

important → more important

12. ④

13. ③

14. The gorilla is the biggest and strongest animal of the apes.

15. ③

16. ④

17. ⑤

tip!

any other islands → any other island

18. the fastest way

19. is (3 years)older than Min (is).

20. is taller than Min (is).

21. Soo is heavier than anyone else.

22. always does better than I do

23. three times more expensive than

24. the, most, diligent

25. as tall as

본문 264 페이지

주니어 고릴라 영문법
Junior Gorilla Grammar 2

핵심만 반복, 그리고 영작!

고릴라 영문법 카페에서
추가 자료와 피드백도 받을 수 있습니다.

2,500여 개의 전국 중학교 기출 문제 및 교과서 완전 분석 후 반영
taborm.com과 고릴라 영문법 카페에서 추가 학습 자료 제공